TADPOLES:
Tiny Tales from Freshwater Adventures

Christina M. Eder

Felicity Press

Copyright © 2021 by Christina M. Eder

Cover by Red Paint Spilman
Interior layout by Rita M. Reali
Final cover implementation by Chris Woods

No portion of this book may be reproduced in any form or by any means, including electronic storage and retrieval systems, without the expressed prior written permission of the author.

All Scripture quotes from *NIV Kids' Adventure Bible.*

When I use the collective "we," "us," "ours," I include myself under that umbrella. This is not intended to categorize, judge, preach or attempt to manipulate the reader to agree or embrace my thoughts.

Connect with Christina on Facebook (www.facebook.com/EDERAuthor).

Eder, Christina M.
TADPOLES: Tiny Tales from Freshwater Adventures

ISBNs:
(paperback) 978-1-7346596-4-1
(ebook)   978-1-7346596-5-8

Printed in the U.S.A.
First American edition, September 2021

Other books by Christina M. Eder:

Life's Too Short for Dull Razors, Cheap Pens, and Worn Out Underwear

The FROG Blog: Learning on a Lily Pad

UNTHAWED: Lessons from a Frozen Lily Pad

KNEE DEEP: A 9-Month Whirlpool of Handwritten Letters to the Creator

Contents

About the Author viii
Acknowledgments ix
In the Beginning 3
Backstory 4
Four-Word Living 6
Look Up! 8
Glass Houses 9
Sunshine and Smiles 11
Alarming Trust 13
Digging for Gold 15
Heightened Awareness 17
I Will Raise You Up on Ostrich Wings? 18
Dressed for Encouragement 20
Turning on a Dime 22
Guilty Plea 23
No Fair-Weather Walking 25
Scratches and Dents 26
A Hard-Boiled Lesson 28
Dressed in a Smile 30
Frugal Makeover 31
Driver's Ed for the Mind 33
Pioneer or Toddler? 35
A Surprise in the Wait 36
Measure Twice, Cut Once. 38
On Second Thought... 40
Lifelong Contract 42
Depth Perception 44
Reliable Transportation 46
One Choice. Eternal Consequences. 48
Listless Awareness 50
A Storybook Quote 52
Surprise Rental 54

Abbreviated Priority 56
On-the-Spot Cleaning 58
Think Orchestra, Not Shotgun 59
Glaze on Cracked Pottery 61
A Do-Si-Do 63
I Am Uzzah 65
Protective Pause.. 67
Boredom is in the Eyes of the Beholder 69
Farmer, Farmer! 71
Thank It Forward 73
A Year of Intent... 75
A Fraction Yields a Whole-Number
    Solution.. 77
Order's Up! 79
Cracked Up.. 81
Anticipate the Unknown.......................... 83
Voice Texts 85
Joyfully Overweight.................................. 87
Beware! 89
Tempered... 91
Jesus: From Introvert to Extrovert 93
Off the Grid or Sheltered? 95
A Great Day. Really? 97
Breaking to Decipher 99
Time's Up 101
Change of Venue..................................... 103
Working on Fallow Ground 105
Growing Potential 107
A Pigheaded Lesson 109
Audio Delusion 111
When I'm 18! 113
Merciful Attire... 115
Recall Notice 117
Incomplete Education 119
Addressing My Distractions 121

Christina M. Eder

Well, I'll Be! 123
What Can I Do Other Than...? 125
Blocked Out 127
Leggo My Eggo! 129

YOUNG CONTRIBUTORS

The Best Relationship
   Katie D. 131

A Changing Leaf
   Irelyn 132

The Healing Power of the Outdoors
   Ben 134

Making Connections Through Music
   Josie E. 135

These Are a Few of My Favorite Things
   Connor 137

God is Mysterious in Many Ways
   Parker E. 139

Look for the Pebbles, Not the Planes
   Sarah G. 141

Faith Your Fears
   Jake I. 143

God Has a Plan
   Aiden J. 145

Using Gifts to Serve Others
  Alia 146

A Memory I Will Cherish for Life
  Breanna L. 148

God Working
  Westley M. 150

Accidental Awakening
  Kali V. 152

About the Author

Christina M. Eder writes with a transparent curiosity from her Martha & Mary Studio in Tennessee. Tutoring aspiring authors and coaching people in transition puts food in her body. Writing feeds her spirit.

You'll discover an inside scoop of Christina's heart both in her books and on her website: www.gueststarcoaching.com.

Acknowledgments

Thank you to all readers and writers of light. In this fourth book of the FROG Blog series, I created *Tadpoles: Tiny Tales from Freshwater Adventures* with a 300-word or less window.

I have few words and abundant gratitude to applaud each person who responded to this project. Some people answered yes. Some answered no. Each of us – author included – responded to this literary invitation with varying levels of uncertainty.

FROG: To Fully Rely On God.

We suited up, dove deep and found treasures packed in lessons and blessin's. We FROG-ged together. Therefore, I dedicate this book to everyone. We're all tadpoles practicing this earthly experience for the first time. Seize every minute with childlike wonder!

With support for your adventure,

Christina M. Eder

TADPOLES:
Tiny Tales from Freshwater Adventures

Christina M. Eder

TADPOLES: Tiny Tales from Freshwater Adventures

In the Beginning...

"As an eagle prepares its young to leave the nest, with all the skills and knowledge it needs to participate in life, in the same manner so will I guide my children. I will use the culture to prepare them for life."
– Native American philosophy.

"Start children off on the way they should go, and even when they are old they will not turn away from it"
(NIV Adventure Bible; ages 9-12 version).

"A child can ask questions that a wise man cannot answer"
– Lakota proverb

Backstory

In roughly 300 words, this is the backstory of *Tadpoles: Tiny Tales from Freshwater Adventures.*

Tadpoles: is book #4 in the FROG Blog book series. This leap from the lily pad comes from a discovery about the value of one. One thought becomes one experience. One experience grows into one pattern. One habit matures into one routine. And one routine becomes a lifetime scrapbook (sometimes scrap-heap worthy, sometimes book worthy). ☺

I have become more aware of stories. People want to share their history. They have insights to leave to the world. To stay within the length of my FROG Blogs, my initial group of FROG Book anthologists wrote their lessons and blessin's within 500 words.

I read statistics regarding diminishing attention spans. In 1998, readers focused for approximately 12 minutes. In 2008, it was five minutes. By 2018, 55 percent read a blog for 15 seconds. To date, that has dropped to an estimated eight-second reader attention span. (For perspective, to a bull rider, eight seconds qualifies as a win)!

Initially I felt downtrodden over this waning-attention statistic. I chose to paddle new waters around the lily pad. I'd decrease my blogs to 300 words to cut through literary swamps. This trimming encouraged me to sharpen my word choices.

While pruning my words, I welcomed a

younger client base within my life-coaching business, thanks to today's virtual-learning trends. Parents wanted their children to get coaching and writing support via phone. Youths were more inclined to speak when not faced with in-person appointments.

One business pattern grew into this book. I invited several teens to capture their life discovery in 300 words. Writing a 300-word snapshot seemed less daunting for them than to write a 500-word essay.

Hence, *Tadpoles* evolved. With messages comparable to those from books like *If You Give a Moose a Muffin*, *Tadpoles'* development follows from literary conception to multiple births.

These stand-alone stories may be viewed as word babies, from God's children growing spiritually.

Cradled in childlike wonder on life's lily pad,

Christina M. Eder

Four-Word Living

"Thank you. I'm sorry."

A retired Air Force pilot used these four words to summarize his beliefs when we sat next to each other on a flight to Knoxville, Tennessee (we were both passengers; I wasn't his co-pilot ☺). He glanced at the *Guideposts* magazine I was reading and said, "Based on that article, I take it you're Christian?"

I simply smiled and answered yes.

He said he's condensed his heavenly conversations into four words: "Thank you" and "I'm sorry." The pilot's few faithful words led to a lengthy conversation about gratitude and humility. He said "thank you" keeps his heart soft and "I'm sorry" reminds him he has much still to learn.

What I learned from that conversation inspired me to live my life differently. Instead of saving or trying to remember prayers for a "better" time, I'll say them immediately. I've incorporated what author Bob Hostetler calls "breath prayers."

Hostetler said he finds he can't always stop at a church or find somewhere to kneel or light a candle. Sometimes it's not appropriately convenient to close his eyes and bow his head, but he can manage breath prayers.

Simple acknowledgment. Short. Easy. Words spoken in a single breath and repeated numerous times throughout the day.

When I include breath prayers into my regular travels, I've noticed a decrease in cabin pressure and elevated awareness. Thank you. I'm sorry. That retired Air Force pilot gave me a four-word reminder. Pray it "four-word."

With mindful simplicity to include God on my frequent-flier destinations,

Christina

"Enter his gates with thanksgiving and his courts with praise; give thanks to him and praise his name" (Psalms 100:4).

"This is how my heavenly Father will treat you unless you forgive your brother or sister from your heart" (Matthew 18:35).

Christina M. Eder

Look Up!

Because of their shorter stature, children looked up to Jesus while He taught when He was on earth. Unlike the people who were trying to silence them, Jesus didn't look down on those wee ones. Thankfully, He doesn't look down on me as an adult-child-in-training.

In Matthew 19:14, Jesus used an unexpected solution to solve a growing problem among the crowd. Instead of leaving children in the background, He told the adults to bring those curious babes to the front of His class. He wanted to teach all children, regardless of age or education level.

People sometimes perceive children as their distractions. Jesus views children of all ages as his attractions. He sometimes delivers adult lessons through minor blessin's. Jesus confers value in how we've increased our spiritual frame rather than how our physical stature has evolved.

In any area of my life, regardless of how low I sink, Jesus invites me to look up to Him. Whatever worldly heights I seek, Jesus invites me to look up to Him. As a daughter of the King, Jesus wants me to always look up to Him.

Small in physical stature, yet growing in FROG leaps and bounds on this lily pad of life,

Christina

"Jesus said, 'Let the little children come to me, and do not hinder them, for the kingdom of heaven belongs to such as these' " (Matthew 19:14).

Glass Houses

I teach seminars about mindfulness. When I need to get a group to become silent, I lightly clink a glass.

One of my mindfulness exercises invites participants to close their eyes and identify an object that matches a sound. Even with their eyes closed, I watch facial expressions associate the chiming sound with my "call-to-attention glass."

I ask them to close their eyes again. This time I tap a glass fishbowl filled with rocks and plastic frogs. Again, their expressions presume they've identified the previous glass with the clinking.

With their eyes still closed, I ask them to describe the object's color, value, purpose and age. Frequently, attendees describe the "call-to-attention" glass. After offering guesses, participants open their eyes to see the fishbowl. (Some want to know why there are plastic frogs instead of fish in the bowl).

Less than 15 minutes into our workshop, guests come to associate that clinking glass with a call to alertness. This is when I present an invitation to consider audio mindfulness.

I hear about somebody. I see someone. I listen and watch. I don't know their history or present circumstances, yet I draw conclusions. Sometimes I shine favorable opinions. Other times, I allow dark assumptions. Only God truly understands past and future with every detail in between.

He knows my thoughts, dreams, fears

and comfort zones. I relate to those plastic frogs in a fishbowl. Earth temporarily houses me to serve God's purpose, but I'm created to leap and swim toward eternal freedom.

God uses His voice to design creations of love. He takes the worst of my past and blends His potential worth to craft someone the world may not imagine.

Creator, please tune my witness to be associated with kindness, the object of Your affection.

Christina

"*What no eye has seen, what no ear has heard, and what no human mind has conceived the things God has prepared for those who love him*" (1 Corinthians 2:9).

Sunshine And Smiles

To protect the innocent, for this FROG Blog, I've changed the name of one of our granddaughters.

Our granddaughter Rhea shared with us how nervous she becomes whenever she faces a new experience. She typically encounters this restlessness after a weekend or extended school break.

She and I talked about how she feels most lonely whenever she passes someone and smiles, or greets someone who doesn't return her greeting. Rhea said that once she gains eye contact, she easily joins in conversation, but she won't speak unless the other person acknowledges her first.

I invited her to create options that could address her uneasiness.

She said, "Grams, I want to do something that takes away my loneliness, but not something where I need to talk to someone."

I told her Jesus is always with her, but she wasn't readily biting on that fact to ease her eight-year-old worry.

Rhea has told me she enjoys walking outside to organize her mind, so I suggested that when she feels alone, she go outside to ask Jesus for a smile. If she cannot go outside, I suggested she go to a window, look up, smile and know Jesus would see her. That solution inspired her to copy what she hears me frequently use as my opening greeting, "Happy Monday (or whatever day it is), friend!"

In addition to her strategic eye contact and smiles, Rhea practices courage with a bright, "Happy Tuesday (or Wednesday, or Thursday), friend!" I'm believing she will gain confidence and uplift others.

With a vibrant outlook on cloudy days from the FROG Blog,

Christina

"So I came out to meet you; I looked for you and have found you!" (Proverbs 7:15).

Alarming Trust

I got my first alarm clock for Christmas when I was 12 years old. That gift represented my rite of passage because, prior to that Christmas, my parents had been responsible for waking me when it was time to start a day.

I saw that gift as a sign that my parents considered me responsible to wake on time and get myself ready. I needed to honor our family's breakfast, shower and transportation schedules, but I wanted to show my parents I was mature enough to be prepared.

In the back of my mind, I knew if I'd overslept or didn't hear the alarm, my parents would provide the necessary backup (although various consequences followed when I forgot to set the alarm or had the volume set too low).

Similarly, in my awakening with God, I've learned consequences result when I don't tune in to His Newscast. And sometimes my frequency is set to follow my own independent broadcast instead of God's daily show. Other times, I don't hear His voice because I'm so focused on my reports and updates.

The staticky frequency fills my air waves with unfocused energy, irritability or restlessness. Those indicators remind me to change channels and turn up God's volume. I need to set my dial to His voice instead of using Him as my backup alarm when emergency news flashes develop.

Like Samuel waking Saul in 1 Samuel 9:26, God calls me to get up and trust Him. He knows where and when we're going, together, every second of the way.

Christina M. Eder

Responding to God's wake-up call,

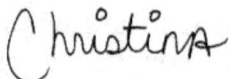

"They rose about daybreak, and Samuel called to Saul on the roof, 'Get ready, and I will send you on your way.' When Saul got ready, he and Samuel went outside together" (1 Samuel 9:26).

Digging For Gold

To protect the innocent, for this FROG Blog, I've changed a granddaughter's name to Gracie, and the school counselor's last name to Jones. But don't let that imply we're trying to keep up with the Joneses!

1 John 3:7 says, "Little children, let no one deceive you. He who practices righteousness is righteous, just as He is righteous." I read this Scripture on a day when my Grams' heart rebelled against Fully Relying On God. Gracie shared a conversation she had with her school counselor that stretched me to silence my inner Grams bear as she relayed the encounter.

Gracie had sought guidance from a trusted school professional regarding a second grader's taunting about nose picking versus nose scratching. (*That* exchange may become one of my comedy routines, but the remaining dialogue is not humorous).

Her counselor asked Gracie to suggest possible solutions to this classmate's teasing. Gracie said when she said she would pray for him, the counselor snickered and asked, "But what *else* could you do?"

Since Gracie had other answer, she stalled for time by asking, "Miss Jones, do you go to church?"

She responded, "I don't believe in God."

I'm unable to expound on that conversation, but I can pass along Gracie's perception that followed. Without hesitation, after relating how the counselor divulged her personal view,

Gracie said, "Grams, I didn't tell Miss Jones this, but maybe I can pray for *her*, too!"

In the time it took for me to get my nose back in joint after hearing this counselor's (un)profession of belief, my granddaughter had already proclaimed her answer. Gracie's battle solution reminded me prayer is the quickest warfare strategy.

Gracie walked to the counselor's office seeking advice. I drove Gracie home reclaiming wisdom through her guidance. God uses every experience, each person – 86,400 seconds of every day – to teach lessons if I am watching for them.

Scratching the surface and picking out truth that is sometimes right in front of my nose,

Christina

"Dear children, do not let anyone lead you astray..." (1 John 3:7).

Heightened Awareness

I consider Zacchaeus a biblical giant. Luke described Zacchaeus as short by comparing his height to the crowd's stature. Zacchaeus' can-do attitude wasn't stunted when he climbed a tree to watch Jesus passing through town.

Zacchaeus was a short tax collector who didn't allow crowd comparisons to stand in front of his determination to see Jesus. He used his tall-enough-to-reach-the-ground legs to run to a higher vantage point.

Zacchaeus' height may have differed from that of a towering crowd, yet they shared a desire to connect with Jesus. Zacchaeus united resourcefulness with anticipation. He created a bird's eye view from a timberline box seat. When Jesus passed beneath Zacchaeus' makeshift skybox, He invited the other man to leave his aerial vantage point so they could share dinner that evening.

Zacchaeus scaled a tree. The Little Engine that could climbed a mountain railway. I stretch on a lily pad of life to learn spiritual lessons. We can stretch. Internally or externally, we can ascend. With God, I know I can, I know I can.

Scaling back and doing what I *can* from the FROG Blog,

Christina

"...there was a man named Zacchaeus... And he sought to see who Jesus was, but could not because of the crowd, for he was of short stature. So he ran ahead and climbed into a sycamore tree to see Him" (Luke 19:2-4).

Christina M. Eder

I Will Raise You Up on Ostrich Wings?

When it comes to birds, I read about sparrows, eagles, doves and the occasional woodpecker nestled in biblical stories. Storks and ostriches typically fly under my radar, but the book of Job flocks toward these two unsung heroes.

I needed to research ostriches and storks. My familiarity with storks was limited to cartoon images on animated baby-delivery announcements. The ostrich was thought to be stupid because of its awkward appearance. This gawky-looking bird is the heaviest bird on the planet and unable to fly; but, capable of reaching land speeds of 60-70 miles per hour, it can outrun a fast horse.

Job 39:13 compares ostrich wings to stork wings, which led to more bird questions. The stork has a full plumage of feathers and warmly uses them to protect their young.

Ostriches, on the other hand (or wing), use their heavy pinions to raise their young in a seemingly hazardous way.

Despite misunderstandings about raising their children with heavy-winged parenting methods, these unsophisticated birds blissfully flap their wings. Their feathers remain unruffled when they're compared to other birds.

The ostrich and stork teach yet another lesson of how God uses tough old (or young) birds to soar in His flight pattern. He doesn't allow weighted wings, assumed lack of intelligence or comparisons to keep Him from crafting the most unlikely people into His wingmen and -women.

    I want to make sure my wings (and beak) flap encouragement so others find themselves elevated during their earthly flight. By using gentle hope, and less "fowl" play, we can all fly friendlier skies.

    Joyfully running among the ostriches on the lily pad,

Christina

    "The wings of the ostrich flap joyfully, though they cannot compare with the wings and feathers of the stork" (Job 39:13).

Dressed For Encouragement

I love being someone's cheerleader, especially when they're starting a new endeavor. I like to use cards, phone calls, Facebook posts, online reviews, walk-and-talk coaching sessions and even cooking to send sunshine onto someone's path.

Truth be told, I selfishly enjoy the uplift I get from doing these things, because I know how valuable I find it when someone believes in my adventures.

But what about dressing to lighten up someone's view? I want my clothes to "speak" brightness. On rainy or cloudy days, I purposely wear my most vibrant-colored blouses. Sometimes I'll catch my own reflection in a mirror or window when I'm wearing pink, lime green or turquoise, and these colors naturally elevate my spirit.

I dress "professionally flexible," so I'm prepared to adapt to daily business or servant roles. During my workday, if I'm wearing what some people may consider a "nice" T-shirt, I feel frumpy and less inclined to be as upbeat. Wearing heavily tailored clothes or heels stifles me. I choose a blend of clothes requiring minimal adjusting and encouraging free-flowing movement.

As a former corporate employee, I was trained to dress for success, according to the business world's definition of achievement. As an author of Light, I train myself to dress for encouragement, which, to me, defines success.

Today I sign off, wearing a purple and vibrant-blue blouse. I seek to create a colorful boost to my lily pad dwellers around the FROG Blog,

Christina

"Therefore encourage one another and build each other up, just as in fact you are doing" (1 Thessalonians. 5:11).

Turning on a Dime

My Grandpa Wes carried dimes in his pockets and whenever he'd take his grandkids outside for a walk, he'd subtly toss a dime in the path of the lagging child. When we'd discover these dimes, he'd tell us these were signs of heaven reaching down. He'd explain when we pay attention to details, we find life's subtle treasures.

I continue Grandpa Wes' dime-tossing tradition when I walk. Each time I drop a coin, I ask God to bring peace and hope to whoever finds it. Like Jesus, who said He left His peace on earth, I want my dropped change to invite a change for whoever finds the coin.

Often, I write about ways I practice keeping my chin up and my eyes fixed on things above. God surrounds me on all levels. Sometimes, in looking down, I find peace if I readily bend to pick up these treasures.

Other times, I find hope simply by looking up to capture a full moon, a soaring bird or a cloud forming an unusual shape. When I am willing to turn on a dime to make a change, I can accept God's abundant peace and hope.

Signing off with peace and hope from the lily pad of life. With bended knee and a coined phrase, "help me pay it forward,"

Christina

"Blessed are those who find wisdom, those who gain understanding, for she is more profitable than silver and yields better returns than gold" (Proverbs 3:13-14).

Guilty Plea

Someone charged me as guilty within the first sentence of a conversation when he began, "I know you're going to be upset when I say this, but..."

I gulped and responded with my best neutral facial expression.

He continued, "I know you're going to be hurt and I'm sure this wasn't your intent, but..."

He went on to cite an email from three weeks prior and summarized his perceived interaction between us. I wasn't present in his inner dialogue, yet he had engaged me in his imaginative response, based on how he figured I'd reply.

His assessment was partially correct, but I was most hurt that he had assumed my reaction before I even detected a miscommunication from three weeks ago.

The sting of this lesson got under my skin because I realized I convict others when I presume their thoughts or motives. For example, I'll think, "I bet he feels pressured when I show up to meetings ten minutes early." Or, "She's probably wondering whether I'm reliable because I didn't call her back sooner."

In Isaiah 55:8, he said God's thoughts and ways are not the same as my thoughts and ways. Any name could replace the "my" and "your" in this passage. "For Suzy's thoughts are not Christina's thoughts," or "Christina's ways are not Tommy's ways."

I practice surrendering to an infallible Creator who thinks and responds differently than I sometimes want. In this way, I relate to my Creator when I struggle with others who expect their solution or pace to match mine.

This email interpretation allowed me to learn a lesson about respecting each other's process. We don't always align, but we can adjust with kind regard. From that conviction, I received a more innocent plea.

Leaping to offer the benefit of the doubt,

Christina

"For my thoughts are not your thoughts, neither are your ways my ways, declares the Lord" (Isaiah 55:8).

No Fair-Weather Walking

Each morning, I walk to the mailbox between 7:30 and 8, when many of my neighbors start their work or school days. As they pass by, I make a point of sending them off with a smile, wave or greeting – "Happy Tuesday" (or whatever day it is).

This morning as I opened our door to take my mailbox stroll, a torrential downpour began. I was tempted to wait until the rain let up, but instead felt nudged to move forward. I figured people might appreciate a smile even more to start a rainy day.

One of my natural habits is to wear brightly colored clothes on cloudy days, and especially Mondays, which often get a harsh rap. Today, I was dressed in a vibrant pink blouse and, as I headed to the mailbox, I grabbed my umbrella.

On my route, I greeted one of my neighbors, who wore a canary-yellow blouse. Before she got into her car, she said, "Between your pink blouse and my yellow one, it looks like we have the same idea – to use color to show positive thinking on this rainy day!"

As I walked home, I realized had I stayed inside until the storm passed, I'd have missed our neighborly ray of sunshine.

Puddle jumping into the day under an umbrella of encouragement,

Christina

"*Now go out and encourage your men*" *(2 Samuel 19:7).*

Christina M. Eder

Scratches And Dents

At the entrance of a parking lot, I noticed a compact car with two moderately sized dents in the body along the driver's side. Even though this car had seen better days, it was still drivable.

And, much like that damaged car, I thought about how we, as earth walkers and drivers, have been injured. We've hurt and been hurt by someone or something that has left bruises. Some scars may show up on our body. But many of our wounds are stored in our hearts.

I don't know the story behind the dented car in that parking lot, but now I've got a new viewpoint to consider. Some people may be like compact vehicles, traveling through life's obstacle course and colliding with multiple barricades. Sometimes smaller cars are better able to avoid these obstructions; but when they do hit one, it can leave more damage than a larger vehicle would sustain when hitting that same obstacle.

The heftier car may hit more blockades but each one incurs less damage than its smaller counterparts. Some folks resemble shiny heavy-duty trucks, but a look at their worn tires indicates they've trod rocky paths.

Today, I see my fellow drivers and passengers through a windshield of universally dented vehicles. We're navigating life's potholes. Sometimes our potholes seem like sinkholes during our commute back Home. I believe those eternal highways will be paved in gold.

Treading with more compassionate strokes around the lily pad of life,

Christina

"Therefore, as God's chosen people, holy and dearly loved, clothe yourselves with compassion, kindness, humility, gentleness, and patience" (Colossians 3:12).

A Hard-Boiled Lesson

I eat hardboiled egg whites and broccoli as my standard breakfast. It's tasty, simple and healthy. This morning while I waited for the egg water to boil, I was quickly constructing my schedule. (A side note: Mentally exercising on an empty stomach leads me to stress fractures!)

Before the kettle was even warm, I had visualized today's writing project and sent it to the editor. In my speedy check-off list, I had bypassed start-to-finish details such as composing the first draft, editing, rewriting and creating a headline.

The egg water hadn't even boiled before I realized I had mentally barged through today as I had expected it to evolve. What if I were to disregard all time, space and interactions this way?

As children, we used to play Backwards Day. We'd wear our pajamas inside-out, eat breakfast for dinner, use our less dominant hand to draw or throw a ball. Those temporary silly days showed me how atypical routines increased my effort and awareness.

Each day is different with God. He respects the shape in which He designed His universe. What would our world look like if carnations grew underground? What if elephants had babies as often as rabbits?

Jesus understood how human nature wants to get a sneak peek at the future. He instructed us to remain on task when He said, "Give us this day, our daily bread." So I am to trust that He'll provide patience, time, people or whatever else I need for that day. Each day.

As I prepared breakfast on the lily pad of the FROG Blog, I respect the steps leading to the meal. Brew coffee. Put eggs and broccoli on plate. Thank God for farmers and food. Eat, and enjoy each breath of every minute crafted into this day.

I'm routinely practicing mindfulness "on earth as it is in heaven,"

"Give us today our daily bread" (Matthew 6:11).

Dressed in a Smile

When I sort my closet, to keep my possessions to a minimum, I use a buy one, get rid of one item approach. I have a turquoise-and-brown dress I bought on clearance at JC Penney over a decade ago.

This past year, I've considered trading this clearance dress for a newer one. I wear it "one more time" with the intent to wash it and donate it afterward. Sure enough, the day I wear it, several people say, "I love your dress!" Comically, that dress has become a discussion starter.

This morning, clothed in my "one more time" JC Penney dress, I walked past a neighborhood gardener. She looked up from her flower bed and exclaimed, "Your dress print makes me happy. I needed to see that today!" I don't know what kind of day she was having or how my dress' design made her smile, but I know her kind words hemmed an uplifting pattern into my day.

When I wear that dress "one last time" I'm never sure whether it's still in style. However, that gardener's response reminded me no matter what is considered fashionable by the world's standards, smiles never go out of style.

Stitching threads of kindness into the fabric of life,

Christina

"...may your priests, Lord God, be clothed with salvation, may your faithful people rejoice in your goodness" (2 Chronicles 6:41).

Frugal Makeover

I want to become a fashion model who is eternally ageless and never goes out of style. To achieve this runway status, maybe the only thing I need is to keep my smile muscles well-toned.

A pleasant facial expression remains a classic fit, no matter what fashion is being modeled. Smiling requires no surgery, a gym membership, an endless bank account or cosmetics. Humans come automatically equipped from the Factory with this unique, no-cost feature. No two smiles are alike, even when they come from the same person!

I became more aware of my own facial expression when a friend told me she'd seen me driving with a look of intensity. She said, "I'm used to seeing you smiling or at least not frowning, but whatever you were thinking sure made your brow furrowed!"

I knew which day she was referring to because I'd had a heavy mind. Based on that moment's facial expression in the car, my demeanor gave an atypical view of my customary personality. I remind myself on rough days it's difficult to be upset when you're smiling.

Some days, my heart needs to race to catch up with my smile, but with thoughtful consideration, eventually the brightness shines through. Thankfully, this person knows me and what my natural demeanor reflects.

What about someone seeing me for the first, or only, time? What impression do I leave them with the tight-lipped expression my friend saw on me when I was driving?

Not all thoughts are lightweight, but if I frequently train my thoughts with repetitive smiles, I receive a no-cost makeover – and a raised spirit. No matter how much exercise my smile gets, it's a classic fit that never goes out of style.

From the lily pad – where my status symbol is my smile,

Christina

"See to it, then, that the light within you is not darkness" (Luke 11:35).

Driver's Ed for the Mind

"At this time tomorrow, you won't be sitting in this same spot."

My mom used to tell me this when I was learning to drive. To teach me about being a patiently kind driver, she'd say, "Christina, at this time tomorrow, you won't be sitting in this same spot."

She'd see me wiggling in the driver's seat, waiting for a red light to turn green and she'd gently say, "Christina, I promise. At this time tomorrow, you won't be sitting in this same spot."

We'd drive among slow-moving traffic through congested rush hours. We got stuck behind school buses and garbage trucks. Each time, Mom repeated her driver's education quote. "Christina, at this time tomorrow you won't be sitting in this same spot."

Sometimes she'd humor me and wager a bet to guess how many hours we'd be at a standstill. There was never a time when we waited more than a few minutes, but any holdup seemed amplified during the delay.

Thirty-five years later, Mom's one-sentence mantra still speaks calm into my fidgeting self. When I'm agitated, I revert to, "Christina, at this time tomorrow, you won't be sitting in this same spot."

My mother's simple reminder helps to direct my traffic pattern on the highway of life. She taught me to mentally apply the brakes whenever my impatience sped me through construction zones that sometimes resembled a *de*construction zone. *Caution. Fines doubled* *in construction zones.*

At this time tomorrow, I plan to continue moving forward. I'll travel the pace I was designed to go. I won't be sitting in this same spot.

Merging toward the front in the center lane,

Christina

"What you heard from me, keep as the pattern of sound teaching, with faith and love in Christ Jesus" (2 Timothy 1:13).

Pioneer or Toddler?

Sometimes I feel like I walk a fine line between being a pioneer or wobbling like a toddler. I'll step into an unknown situation with an adventurous spirit, eager to explore every inch of earth. Other times, my less enthusiastic self may approach the world with trepidation.

Pioneers and toddlers both venture into uncharted territory, invited to choose trust or timidity. I can determine much of my growth, survival and accomplishment rate based on which route I travel.

If I give up on God's plans, it allows fear of the unknown (or known) to win. Steering toward my Creator's path leads to triumph. I recall seeing a quote about achievement that said, "Success is like riding a bicycle. Either you keep moving or you fall over."

On the trail to eternal perfection, some days I'm hopping on a mountain bike to ride a rugged course. Other times I'm pedaling a tricycle or wobbling on training wheels. Provided I'm not backpedaling, I'll pioneer my way to an Eternal Trail, one rotation at a time.

Forging wholeheartedly into sometimes-unknown territory. Trusting the Founding Father who blazes this trail for my life. Seeking landmarks of courage,

Christina

"At that time I will search Jerusalem with lamps and punish those who are complacent... who think, 'The Lord will do nothing, either good or bad' " (Zephaniah 1:12).

A Surprise in the Wait

I often choose the longest checkout lane at a business. Yes, the longest lane. This buys my supply of free entertainment via customer interaction, browsing magazines and checking out candy flavors or shelved trinkets.

One day, my only option at the post office was an extended line. People were using their wait time to check their phones, crowd watch and peruse the limited reading material. (Even advertisements for the various mailing options become a precious reading commodity at the post office).

I anticipated a heavy workload that day, so I chose to check phone messages. Instead of feeling relieved about lightening my to-do list by multi-tasking, I grew impatient. The line seemed to lengthen as I grew agitated at listening to numerous phone messages. So, instead of multi-tasking, I found myself multi-taxing.

I had already spread myself too thin. Through my increased activity, I decreased my efficiency. By the time I realized I had created self-made trauma, I was next in line. I spent the remaining wait time to focus on John Wayne's quote: "Talk low. Talk slow. Don't talk too much."

Short message, long-line lesson. One message at a time. One task at a time,

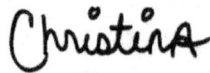

"But Martha was distracted by all the preparations that had to be made. She came to

him and asked, 'Lord, don't you care that my sister has left me to do the work by myself? Tell her to help me!' 'Martha, Martha,' the Lord answered, 'you are worried and upset about many things, but few things are needed – or indeed only one.' " *(Luke 10:40-41).*

Christina M. Eder

Measure Twice, Cut Once.

Measure twice, cut once. My dad taught me this carpenter's rule of thumb. I'd watch him in his workshop and before he reached for his saw, he'd grab his tape measure, level and square.

Dad made an elaborate display of double checking his measuring tape and examining angles. He'd step back for a broad view of his mission and, only after one more inspection, would he finally introduce the saw blade to the material.

Just for good measure, he would glance at me with the reminder, "Measure twice. Cut once." When he pieced the perfect cut (almost always) into his project he'd repeat, "Measure twice. Cut once."

I nailed Dad's carpentry lesson into the woodwork of my daily guideposts. I implement his verbal bookends as I pause before I speak. Think (at least) twice, speak once. I find when I carefully measure word weight, angles and content, my speech is less sharp. I reduce my cutting remarks whenever I use a "think twice, speak once" framework.

Thanks to a Google search, I found in 1984, British writer, actor, broadcaster, self-professed Word Person and Scrabble fanatic Gyles Brandreth came up with one estimate that the average person speaks 860,341,500 words in a lifetime. (I'm unsure of his mathematical calculations, but Brandreth was so certain his estimate was correct, he included it as the subtitle for his book, *The Joy of Lex: How to Have Fun with 860,341,500 Words).*

I've come to realize – through a process of detailed preparation – I've begun to make higher-quality choices in my words. This discovery is part of what led me to this *Tadpoles* collection in the *FROG Blog* series. Instead of writing lessons from the lily pad in 500 words or less, I measured my thoughts twice and cut my words to 300 once (after intricate editing).

Serving the Master Carpenter one encouraging word at a time,

Christina

"...For the mouth speaks what the heart is full of. But I tell you that everyone will have to give an account on the day of judgment for every empty word they have spoken" (Matthew 12:34, 36).

On Second Thought...

In 2018, I declared my intention to become a published author. I felt I'd wasted 45 years chasing logical living and burying my writing talent. I forfeited more than that if I allowed regret to enter my story.

I read how the prophet Habakkuk was devastated when he got a vision about the violent destruction stemming from people's lack of repentance. In Habakkuk 3:2, he pleaded with God to revive His work from those lost years. Habakkuk changed his cry from "Why does God allow it?" to "Who is this God who will sustain me in the things He allows?"

I feared God was disappointed by my delayed response. When I was in middle school, He'd called me to write. I worried He wouldn't give me publishing opportunities that had been offered because I chose "secure" jobs that offered direct deposit. I trusted world employment more than God's ideal appointment. I was naïve to His mercy.

When I traded a standard business job for my writing studio, God slowly granted me abundance. He didn't allow an easy beginning or a rapid success rate. **GRADUALLY**, He introduced me to coaching clients. He allowed me to practice writing for small publications.

During a drizzling build, He rained showers of wisdom, education and ideas for assignments. Now, with a business growth spurt, I'm learning to rely on His guidance to prioritize projects according to His allotted pace and timelines.

This *Tadpoles* collection will be my

fourth published book in three years' time. I know there are at least seven books after this one. I direct my focus to write from this day forward and trust God to redeem time and sustain my energy.

Leaping with gratefulness for second thoughts and double vision on the lily pad,

Christina

"Lord, I have heard of your fame; I stand in awe of your deeds, Lord. Repeat them in our day, in our time make them known; in wrath remember mercy" (Habakkuk 3:2).

Lifelong Contract

I reflected on three roles I've worked in the business world. In my responsibilities as employer, coworker and employee, I value similar characteristics. I require timelines and resilience. I appreciate an open mind, blended with discernment and honesty.

As I continued to define my employable standards, I added compliance without a need to understand every detail. I also admire a quest to lean into explorative learning curves.

In reviewing my lengthy list, I realized how my heavenly hope of meeting every benchmark was unrealistic and candidly ruthless. If God kept an evaluation sheet, I wonder what He'd include for His "perfect employee." I presume God's list would include willing obedience at the top of His list.

While Jesus was employed on earth, He wore many hats (and sandals). At 12 years old, He was teaching in a Jerusalem temple while His parents rode home after the Passover festival.

After three days of searching, they found Jesus, and Mary expressed concern during their journey to find him. She and Joseph were saddled with anxiety, but Jesus simply responded, "I must be about my Father's business" (Luke 2:49). He knew His job was to faithfully conduct God's business.

God is eternally in the market for quality workers. He has an assignment for me and before I receive a permanent contract in heaven, I need to finish my temporary earthly contract. He doesn't anticipate perfection, but He does expect development of an excellent spirit.

I wonder what my employee review would look like if I compared my list to God's desires for His business. How consistently do I show up for a day's work with timeliness, subordination, resilience, trust without understanding...?

Clocking in on God's timeline to open my mind for His business,

"Didn't you know I had to be in my Father's house?" (Luke 2:49).

Depth Perception

During an eye exam, my ophthalmologist increased my prescription to specially crafted progressive bifocal lenses. He enthusiastically diagnosed this visual deterioration like I had qualified for an upgrade.

This highly functional necessity came with a magnified cost. The far-sighted price didn't allow my budget the luxury of buying a spare pair for hypothetical rescue searches (perhaps for an unnamed lady who removes her facial accessory, walks away and forgets where she left them).

I had gotten into a habit of putting my glasses on and taking them off according to what I was looking at. The doctor said to allow a few weeks to adapt to these new specs, but to keep wearing them.

During this adjustment phase, my gait and equilibrium suffered. My stomach adopted a perpetual queasiness and I had a constant low-level headache. My pocketbook was temporarily compromised, so that insight alone encouraged me to wear my glasses until I went to bed.

When I rely on physical vision over wise depth perception, I experience temporary blindness. I become near-sighted when my agenda blocks a wider scope of reference. This tunnel vision can lead to a path of coldheartedness and an abrasive spirit (another hypothetical example from previously mentioned unnamed lady).

Ecclesiastes 7:25 teaches me to apply my heart to search for wisdom and reason.

Some earthly encounters aren't logical, yet I look for wisdom beyond what I can see.

I've seen that when I allow my nose to become disjointed over life's circumstances, I end up with cross-eyed vision (glasses don't fit well on a disjointed nose, no matter what prescription is in the lens).

Every minute becomes a visual screening. When I respect and follow my Eternal Ophthalmologist's diagnosis for the clearest image, I can walk sure-footed on a progressive path.

Seeking wisdom before making a spectacle of myself,

Christina

"He has blinded their eyes and hardened their hearts, Lest they should see with their eyes, Lest they should understand with their hearts and turn, So that I should heal them" (John 12:40).

Christina M. Eder

Reliable Transportation

When I make my annual hometown visit, I usually fly, because 850 miles separates me from much of my family. On my last trip, I considered the notion to purchase a one-way flight and choose alternative transportation to travel home again.

I considered a train, bus, or car for the return trip. My sense of adventure quickly dwindled when I reviewed my transportation choices: limited schedules, geographically inconvenient stations, higher ticket costs and lengthier travel times.

Conveniently, logic won the bid. I chose the round-trip flight to visit family. Not long afterward, while I was walking, I saw a man trekking the trail using exercise poles. Another exerciser behind him rode a bike. Later, a runner passed me on this greenway.

At the end of my walk, all four of us ended up in the same parking lot. We finished our jaunts in the same place, even though we had different methods of arriving there. A runner, a cyclist, an exercise-pole walker and me. We had the same destination but we chose various methods to get us from Point A to Point B. We passed each other separately, but discovered our paths ended in the same place.

In 1 John 5:13, he teaches that all who believe in God will have eternal life. As a believer, I see life resembling a vast greenway walk. On earth we make different choices, face various circumstances and meet numerous people; yet our intersections eventually lead to an Eternal Parking Lot.

Believing our paths will connect at the Eternal Greenway,

Christina

"*I write these things to you who believe in the name of the Son of God so that you may know that you have eternal life*" (1 John 5:13).

One Choice.
Eternal Consequences.

You only live once – or YOLO, as popularly advertised.

I talked with someone who embraces a YOLO framework. She enters a risky pursuit, and exclaims, "YOLO!" It intrigued me when she questioned my eternal beliefs.

She asked why I believe in temporary bodies and perpetual souls. My short-version response, "If you believe in Jesus, you live on both sides of eternity. In heaven, I read that you'll have a different upgraded form."

She responded, "I want adventures now in case there isn't somewhere else or something better after I die."

She remained apprehensive with my life approach, so I shared insight from a teacher who said, "Live as if there is a heaven. When you die, you can't take prizes *for* yourself, but you can leave prizes *of* yourself. These prizes include laughter, encouraging words, work ethic, smiles and loving spirit."

I believe I'll receive a forever prize package that exceeds any treasures I acquire here on earth. Any temporal possessions I'll leave include monetary debt: buildings to maintain, closets to sort, cars to insure.

I love my beneficiaries too much to "gift" them with a possession-crammed storage shed or garage that needs to be cleaned after I move to heaven. I prefer to leave behind lighthearted memories and values.

This lady and I ended our conversation

with positive observations. I explained how the minimalist in me intertwines with the YOLO in her. When my birth certificate expires, she'll be able to pursue her life adventure because she won't be spending time sorting my lifetime belongings.

One life to swim toward golden ponds,

Christina

"*They will perish, but you remain; they will wear out like a garment. Like clothing you will change them and they will be discarded. But you remain the same, and your years will never end*" *(Psalms 102:26-27).*

Listless Awareness

January often marks a time of revision. It can become an invitation to replace old habits and outdated items with updated learning and new goals.

During Christmas and New Year's, I review career plans, calendar, travel ideas and dreams. This past February, I decided to cut out inventorying much of my life. Forty-plus years of tracking money, time, personal connections and accomplishments. Chopped out. Cold turkey.

My original purpose for these carefully documented strategies was to streamline my efforts. I wanted to track productivity to make sure I used all my resources wisely. By heavily monitoring details, I became preoccupied with the thrill of finishing rather than an awareness of the activity.

Planning and evaluating is useful. However, through over-calculating, this burden diminished the simplicity I sought to develop. I began practicing a "think-once, write-once, leave it all to God" pattern (some thoughts can become repeat offenders, and I don't catch them all on the first mental go-round).

Before morning quiet time, I allow five minutes maximum to write whatever is renting mind space. I stand up to jot these potential distractions because I discovered that when I sit to write "brain dumps," I overthink them and become stuck.

After five minutes, I stash the list under a stack of books and ask God to decode those musings. I wait at least 24 hours to review the memos and am surprised to see how one day can reshape my priorities. I've noticed how a slower response time increases my natural resolution.

Initially, this listless strategy created exactly that. Listlessness. Without my frequently referenced planner, I experienced restlessness. I didn't have a concrete document to reference. I kept appointment logs but feared I'd forget something important. Gradually, I began to review my lists less often and assess them on Fridays only.

Sometimes my former enlistment habit creeps back, but I'm learning God provides wisdom, foresight and memory that isn't found on paper.

In a more peaceful outline,

Christina

"A person's steps are directed by the Lord. How then can anyone understand their own way?" (Proverbs 20:24).

A Storybook Quote

In her book, *When God Doesn't Fix It: Lessons You Never Wanted to Learn, Truths You Can't Live Without,* Laura Story wrote: "When God calls you to something, and you say 'no,' that's disobedience. But when God calls you to one thing and you do three things halfway, that's disobedience as well."

Freewill is a gift and responsibility. Each freewill follower has a choice to build everlasting value or fleeting worthlessness.

I'm in a perpetual state of waiting – for something or someone. This continual waiting room makes it evident God is not ruled by a worldly clock or appointments.

He knows if I received all His lessons and blessin's at once, I would forget some or become overwhelmed by their power.

I trust He uses elapsed time in order for me to slowly discover what He created me to become.

In 1 Corinthians 3:10, Paul teaches that everyone is to build with care. To me, this care includes consistent excellence, especially in a culture that values shortcuts and honors efficiency.

To restate Laura Story, "When God calls you to something, and you say 'no,' that's disobedience. But when God calls you to one thing, and you do three things halfway, that's disobedience as well."

I want to surround myself with sincere and selfless people. I believe my Creator wants and anticipates my sincere selfless acts of obedience, founded with care.

Building from a foundational lily pad of lessons,

Christina

"By the grace God has given me, I laid a foundation as a wise builder, and someone else is building on it. But each one should build with care" (1 Corinthians 3:10).

Christina M. Eder

Surprise Rental

When my husband and I listed our house for sale, we liberally sorted our possessions. After 20 years of home ownership, we sold the American-dream fallacy and decided to rent.

I am a minimalist. By marriage, Tig has adapted to minimalism. Our material sifting during the house sale preparation was... well, minimal. (We'd have a "much difrerent experience" if we were packing Tig's garage on the land we own)!

We moved to a townhouse complex and met a few of our neighbors. Tig and I share an appreciation for being social minimalists. We can be friendly neighbors without engaging in party invitations. Shortly after moving in, I met a retired neighbor who's also a published author. Despite my introverted nature, she and I connected.

Bettye Jean and I exchanged books and short conversations until she moved in to an assisted-living facility. I visited her often in her new home and gradually the time between our communication increased. Bettye Jean and I are what our granddaughter calls "short-term friends." These are friends she meets once at a park or only one birthday party.

Tig and I have had quiet and considerate neighbors. We've had noisy, rude neighbors. I've learned during five years of renting that, unlike Tig and me, many of these occupants aren't long-term residents. This observation has taught me to appreciate the easier-to-love people while becoming less irritated with the "minimally polite" tenants.

I'm surprised what renting has taught me about detaching. I watch heavily packed moving vehicles being laboriously unloaded. The movers look exhausted and many ask why they keep so much stuff.

I reflect on my temporary deployment to earth and ponder heaven's victory. Renting supports my longstanding value to focus on eternal consequences. I appreciate that *less* filling is sometimes more *full* filling.

Flowing with a free spirit toward Larger Oceans,

Christina

"*...and the wise heart will know the proper time and procedure*" *(Ecclesiastes 8:5).*

Abbreviated Priority

Large crowd. Short tax collector. Tall shade tree. Jesus used these three sizeable pieces to utilize all capacities to complete His mission.

In Zacchaeus' story, Jesus features this short tax collector who is watching Him from a tree. Because of Zacchaeus' creative accountant reputation, he most likely didn't have many friends voluntarily saving him a front-row seat at ground level to greet Jesus. But Zacchaeus modeled Jesus' steadfast example. He didn't allow his limited height or crowd respect to hinder him. (Who knows? Zacchaeus may have believed money grows on trees and he was seeking extra income in that tree to supplement his shady tax practice).

Sycamore trees are known to be large and shady, ironically resembling Zacchaeus' thriving business. The tree provided a vantage point for Zacchaeus to witness Jesus with the rest of the crowd. Even though Zacchaeus was hidden, when Jesus arrived at that tree, he stopped walking and looked up. One tree. One road. One man.

Jesus implements His signature style when He magnifies small details. He frequently calls me out of hidden places to join Him in His work. Hiding places vary and may be masked behind fear of something or someone unfamiliar to me.

Jesus sometimes requests immediate action when He invites me to engage in an assignment. He did the same thing to Zacchaeus. Jesus told him to hurry and come down from the tree because He was having dinner at his house.

Like Zacchaeus, I am short. I watch for ways to maximize my height, voice and prompt obedience to respond to Jesus' invitations.

Valuing small details on the lily pad,

Christina

"A man was there by the name of Zacchaeus; he was a chief tax collector and was wealthy. He wanted to see who Jesus was, but because he was short he could not see over the crowd. So he ran ahead and climbed a sycamore-fig tree to see him, since Jesus was coming that way. When Jesus reached the spot, he looked up and said to him, 'Zacchaeus, come down immediately. I must stay at your house today.' " (Luke 19:2-5).

On-the-Spot Cleaning

Tig and I recently miscommunicated our roles in a collaborative project. Interestingly, this interaction that led to harsh retorts happened right before my morning quiet time.

Typically, after my husband and I "share words of intense fellowship," we disengage and let our internal pressure cooker simmer before we talk again. Often that delay provides clarity because we've extinguished our emotional truth. When the fire of the disagreement has lessened, we can have a healthier temperance to make amends.

Matthew 5:25 reminds us to settle matters quickly. Scripture indicates no timeframe for what quickly means. Sometimes an immediate resolution is best; other times, a pause restores a gentler perspective.

In relationships, when I promptly settle matters of the heart, I experience freedom sooner. (When tensions are high, I think it's often easier said than done!) Selfishness cakes onto the insides of my spirit when I hold onto offenses. When I wipe forgiveness across my verbal cutting board, there's less chance of permanent stains.

Polishing my kinder responses and hanging my laundry list of lessons out to dry,

Christina

"Settle matters quickly with your adversary" (Matthew 5:25).

Think Orchestra, Not Shotgun

I was created to write. The world beckons me to market. I write today's FROG Blog between my third and fourth published books.

I am eager to write reflections from my heart. I'm excited to share stories and, after many gritty edits, I appreciate the finished product. I want my craft to be discovered through natural conversation flow, not a fixed venue.

The best tip I read about book promotion is, "Think orchestra, not shotgun." Simple to read, easy to understand. It's difficult to apply when marketers encourage mass shootings from a shotgun platform approach.

I'm hard pressed to dance to an orchestra when surrounded by shotgun blasts. I'm unsettled by publicizing strategies because I prefer energy to come from a beautifully harmonious symphony. I strain to hear a melody over network noise.

In Acts 5:29, Peter said, "We must obey God rather than human beings." In Acts 5:36-39, the story describes Theudas, who claimed to be somebody, and 400 men rallied to him. Later, he was killed, his followers dispersed and his magnificent claims were denied.

After Theudas, Judas, the Galilean appeared and led people to revolt. He was killed and guess what? His followers scattered, too. This Scripture was written pre-mass media.

Acts 5:39 concludes, "Leave these men go... if their activity is of human origin, it will fail. But if it is from God you will not be able to stop these men; you will only find yourselves fighting against God."

I work to write value without the selfish motives. I'm adapting to various marketing suggestions and growing to believe God will advertise His heart song for me.

Changing keys and conducting my mind to tune my ear to hear God's cues,

Christina

"Peter and the other apostles replied, 'We must obey God rather than human beings.' " (Acts 5:29).

Glaze on Cracked Pottery

You know those times when you feel out of sorts or off kilter? Those are the days when you may see the trees in full bloom, but you focus instead on the trunk's rough and brittle bark. It seems I discover life's answers mostly through irony.

I awoke this morning with a lingering heaviness from a conversation last evening. I was determined to outsmart – or avoid – my disappointing recap, so I chose a brightly printed outfit to combat the dark and ever-encroaching blues. My coffee was strong, and my shower was warm; unfortunately, my heart was neither strong nor warm.

In Proverbs 26:23 the author compared an evil heart and enthusiastic lips to a glaze over cracked pottery.

I went through the day, receiving plenty of compliments about my new haircut and my outfit. But this sugar-coated outside couldn't begin sweeten the moldy material inside.

I write today's FROG Blog at the end of my workday. Tonight, I traded my brightly colored work clothes for a white T-shirt with some light stains. The T-shirt is comfortable and humbly acceptable for home, but I would not wear it in public.

I wear my heart on my sleeve and I strive to make it blemish free.

Tonight, though, my spirit has softened, and this T-shirt reminds me it had been white before life's spills left marks. I can recall some of the stories behind those stains, but I invite myself to appreciate the salvageable soft white cotton.

    Scrubbing silver into my daily armor,

Christina

    "Like a coating of silver dross on earthenware are fervent lips with an evil heart" (Proverbs 26:23).

A Do-Si-Do

A handful of topics trigger my hot buttons. I have a history of asking these discussion starters even though I've frequently discovered the answers leave me agitated. It's like a love-loathe tango.

Even though I receive disagreeable (to me) responses, I invite these angst-promoting questions to the conversational dance floor. Somehow, I expect a new melody from the same song, yet still walk away from a fox trot with aching feet.

To cut in on my self-traumatizing Hokey Pokey, I turn myself around...

I waltz over to ask God to teach me His dance steps for healthy living. I *intend* to be a compliant student. He asks me to follow His lead, but when I dance to the beat of my own heart, I imagine He's auditioning for patience while I try out for my eternal encore.

Jesus delivers a perfect presentation of obedience through His example in the Garden of Gethsemane. Before He went to the Cross, Jesus had a hot-topic question for His Father. He asked God three times if there might be an alternative for saving His people that wouldn't require the crucifixion step.

God said no three times, so Jesus finally responded, "I have brought You glory on earth by finishing the work You gave me to do" (John 17:4).

He was a diligent student on earth who stayed in step with His Master, even when He was difficult to follow.

I believe I can update some of my dance

moves when I practice following God's guidance. I'm grateful He allows me an earthly dress rehearsal to prepare for heaven.

Winding my song and steps around the ballroom of life,

Christina

"I have brought You glory on earth by finishing the work You gave me to do" (John 17:4).

I Am Uzzah

I relate to Uzzah. In 2 Samuel 6:1-11, Uzzah is the man struck dead when he touched the Ark of God. God gave David specific instruction for transporting the Ark on poles, not by hand.

David and 30,000 men were delivering the Ark to Jerusalem when the oxen pulling the cart stumbled. Uzzah, walking beside the Ark's cart, violated God's hands-off policy as he reached out to steady it (or so he thought).

I like to believe he instinctively grasped for the Ark, to prevent its falling. God thought otherwise. Because of disobedience, Uzzah instantly died at the touch of God's hand.

People (present company included) are to show respect for God by doing exactly what He says, not by doing what we think would be better. My Creator gave me wisdom, a sound mind and a free will. I get to choose to utilize these gifts to make responsible decisions, according to God's leadership.

The story of Uzzah reminds me when God has given guidelines and I take matters into my own hands, consequences follow. Thankfully, I haven't been struck dead as a result of poor choices. Through Uzzah's story, I'm reminded of the essence of respecting all of God's direction.

Keeping my eyes on the trail and both hands around God's will,

Christina

"When they came to the threshing floor of Nakon, Uzzah reached out and took hold of the ark of God, because the oxen stumbled. The

Christina M. Eder

Lord's anger burned against Uzzah because of his irreverent act; therefore, God struck him down, and he died there beside the ark of God" (2 Samuel 6:6-7).

Protective Pause

Sigh.

A pause. Sometimes a sigh is audible, often coupled with exasperation or weariness. Sometimes sighing can indicate a cleansing breath.

I always appreciate sighs birthed from amazement, like when I treat myself to dark-chocolate almonds or an extended visit to a candle shop.

Whatever generates my breather, Psalms 4 teaches me to stop and search my heart, to be silent. Its context references fear, but I've noticed whenever I silently search my motive before I speak, I tend to receive time-lapsed protection. Sometimes those words need to be silenced in my head before a thought becomes unfavorable.

Silent pauses, when used for tempering and not manipulation, can guard against rash thoughts or actions. Francis Bacon said, "Silence is the sleep that nourishes wisdom."

And Leonardo da Vinci said, "Nothing strengthens authority so much as silence."

Many of my virtue-building heroes speak extremely little. Hollywood created wise sages like Mr. Miyagi from *The Karate Kid*, Yoda from *Star Wars*, and Lieutenant John Dunbar in *Dances with Wolves*. Their character represents people who frequently practice wide berths of silence. They observe generously and speak economically.

Like these habitually silent mentors, I'm investing in a verbal budget. Whenever I feel tempted to max out my verbal credit card, I recall Will Rogers' statement, "Never miss a good chance to shut up."

Taking a deep cleansing breath before diving from the lily pad of life,

"Tremble and do not sin; when you are on your beds, search your hearts and be silent" (Psalms 4:4).

Boredom is in the Eyes of the Beholder

"It's so boring!"

People who've traveled across the Midwest sometimes refer to the trip as unexciting. Whenever I tell people I'm traveling there from Tennessee, I hear, "That sounds dull" or "How monotonous." Sometimes people jokingly ask, "You're going to the Midwest on purpose?"

I refrain from defending its captivating greens, clear air, large horizons and appreciation for farm animals (including the earthy scent of manure). Even though I shiver when temperatures drop below my comfortable 80°, I'm fascinated by the snow-kissed fields and glittering ice formations.

I'm grateful my eyesight allows me a view of wide-open scenery. I'm thankful what some consider 'boring land' gives farmers a countryside that produces my food. I wonder what God thinks when someone describes His artwork as dull, uninteresting or dreary. What if they use those words to define my creations or ideas? I need to remember the value of these things is determined and set by God, not by people.

Eleven million people visited the Great Smoky Mountains last year. Mountains – along with deserts, canyons and valleys – are voted as the best sights in the world. This life invites me to experience all terrain. However, when I face emotionally high or low altitudes, I plead for level fields. Yes, it's true: this same person who's wholly content to walk on steady emotional ground pursues earthly travel into rugged geographical regions.

I have a Travel Guide who knows every bit of earth's landscape like the back of His hand. For eternity, He's led countless tourists around the world. Provided I'm not a backseat driver, I can anticipate joy from His mapped-out adventure.

From a sightseeing trip on the lily pad, across worldwide ponds,

"for every animal in the forest is mine, and the cattle on a thousand hills. I know every bird in the mountains, and the insects in the fields are mine" (Psalms 50:10-11).

Farmer, Farmer!

Based on this morning's experiences, if I used an emoji to describe my reaction, I'd picture a straw-hatted farmer wearing a puckered-up expression. The pucker-up isn't a kissing sort, but more like I-just-sucked-the-juice-out-of-a-truckload-of-lemons-that-life-keeps-dropping-at-my-doorstep.

    I've tolerated allowing one single spore of disappointment to develop into a fully grown root of resentment. And, instead of digging up and discarding this Venus flytrap, I've fed it daily, frequently checking its progress. Sadly, its bitter stems are growing.

    I've come to mistrust someone who is close to me. She has promised much with little follow through. I've allowed her sparse harvest from well-meaning word seeds to flood my crop with pity-party tears. After months of this pattern, I've distanced myself from our plotted field of dreams.

    My injured response is to light the field on fire and burn the bridge. Instead, I need to inspect the hulls of my heart and kindly tend to this relational corn maze.

    In low-lying floodplains, I invite God to clear my bitter stones and replant His seeds of love. I can choose to grow in His forgiveness or become root-bound with heart thorns. I need to accept that my Farmer will protect this relationship from further crop damage. I sign off with a promise to mend this fence today.

    Seeking organic deliverance from rocky soil on the FROG Farm,

Christina

Christina M. Eder

"Be kind to one another, tenderhearted, forgiving one another, even as God in Christ forgave you" (Ephesians 4:32).

Thank It Forward

Thank you for your patience. Thank you for waiting. Thanks for understanding. I've recently learned the value of a grateful introduction.

I was seated in a crowded restaurant. Service was slower than I had anticipated. My hungry impatience was suppressed when the server approached and smiled.

He said, "Hello, friend! Thank you for being patient while you waited."

What? Friend? Thank you? He presumed I had been waiting calmly. I expected a harried server. I anticipated a weary, sometimes-defensive explanation that often follows an apology such as, "Sorry, my manager didn't schedule enough people." Or "We're short staffed" (not referring to height-related shortcomings).

Sometimes an apology is necessary. Sometimes a "thank you" won't be a cure-all. I used this server's food-for-thought strategy in discussing a conflict with a staff member. I started our conversation with, "Thank you for making time to meet and to fully listen to my interpretation of this situation. Your help will speed up our compromise."

The coworker reacted with a mixed response. He had a blank expression, followed by a shocked stare, then an upward glance, as if to ask the ceiling, "Where do I go from here?" He regained his professional composure and I was relieved this gracious discussion opener ended with a mutually benefitting resolution.

Opening my menu of life to a page of thankfulness can lead to healthy options. I'll serve gratitude as my main course of action, dishing it out as an entrée, not an appetizer. I believe its nutritional value will be supersized to encourage others.

Filling my platter of life lessons around freshwater ponds and lily pad leaves,

"A gentle answer turns away wrath, but a harsh word stirs up anger" (Proverbs 15:1).

A Year of Intent

I dubbed the year 2018 my Year of Intent. I'd committed to living with such intent I would be willing to live in a tent so I could do what I was designed to do.

I know I was created to write. Instead of declaring for journalism, communications or English in college, I majored in practical logic. I defaulted to graduate with a business administration-personnel degree.

After 35 years of pragmatic living, my spirit led me back to what it was crafted to be. I had allowed earth's minor priorities to dictate my heavenly major. I heard how so many people yearned to create, but in their artistic practice of learning life, they became molded.

I understood that. And I craved to paint in vibrant colors across dull, boring, ordinary ledger pads.

With a canvas of ideas, I set off to meet my writing love. Gradually, job hunting overpowered soul searching. I pounded pavement, yet dismissed the pounding of my own heart. When reality knocked at my door, I squinted through my peephole of logic.

As I looked through cracks of potential discomfort, I envisioned pain. Athletes get hurt. Managers have employees leave. Artists are underpaid. Dancers get their toes stubbed. Authors get overlooked. Moms' hearts break. Dads grow weary. Investors declare bankruptcy. My spirit was overdrawn.

I'm learning to open windows and open doors of the writing possibilities I find that are already at my doorstep. And when I reflect on the screens of my soul, I gain clarity for what God sees and wants from His craftsmanship.

In five years or in five minutes, will my major concern become a minor incident? Sometimes what I temporarily label as poor timing results in an eternally rich opportunity. My mind lives with intent. (But, thankfully, my earthly body hasn't required any long-term residence in a tent).

Writing from a lily pad on a freshwater FROG Blog,

Christina

"Do not lay up for yourselves treasure on earth, where moth and rust destroy..." (Matthew 6:19).

A Fraction Yields a Whole-Number Solution

According to beepods.com, the average bee will make a twelfth of a teaspoon of honey in its lifetime. As a human bee-ing, I'm stung with the thought of leaving the earth with a twelfth of a teaspoon of honey as my lifetime legacy.

Beepods.com also states there's only one queen bee in a colony of 40,000-60,000 bees during spring or early summer. Within human colonies, this queen bee could be described as a woman of clout.

A honeybee visits 50-100 flowers during a single nectar-collection journey. In earthly business, I envision that as attending 50-100 trade shows or making 50-100 client connections in one trip.

One third of all food Americans eat is derived from some source of honeybee pollination. Where would I be without these diligent worker bees? Their job performance teaches me they are fulfilling what they are created to do.

Am I completing what my heavenly King Bee asks of me? If I knew my life would produce only one twelfth of a teaspoon of honey, would I be satisfied? If I were Queen Bee, how would I lead a staff of 40,000-60,000? Could I handle 50-100 collection calls and, at the end of the trip, return with a puny drop of honey in the bucket?

God has a role for everyone. In 1 Corinthians 3, I read about everybody having a role. One waters, one plants, one gathers, but only

God grows their offering. Every job, every person is an essential worker to God. He could run the universe on His own, yet He chooses to invite us to join Him.

I'm humbled that a Being who created everything, and who needs nothing, wants my everything. Whether I'm queen bee or honeybee, I want to be His worker bee.

Buzzing around the lily pad on a wing and a prayer,

Christina

"So neither the one who plants nor the one who waters is anything, but only God, who makes things grow. The one who plants and he one who waters have one purpose, and they will each be rewarded according to their own labor. For we are co-workers in God's service; you are God's field, God's building" (1 Corinthians 3:7-9).

TADPOLES: Tiny Tales from Freshwater Adventures

Order's Up!

Toxic? Sanitary? Is what I'm serving others worthy of a health-department inspection? On a 100-point scale, would a score of 99 even be acceptable? That depends on the scorekeeper.

Restaurants are required to post their food-safety reports. I glance at these reviews, usually *after* I've placed my food order. How would my health score compare to God's assessment?

When I'm cooking, is kindness the first ingredient I reach for? Do I feed my family with the same compassion I serve guests? If I roast spicy grudges or bitter herbs into my life recipe, they become poison to whoever eats my cooking.

Regrettably, I sometimes stir unequal parts of justice and grace. I crave justice for others, yet hunger for grace for myself.

I am created to serve my Master and I remain open for His 24/7 business. I need to use a perpetual cleaning cycle to release stained thoughts (a form of brainwashing I need to sometimes run on its heaviest setting). My motives require frequent filter changes.

I prepare for my Honored Guest when my head is covered in a peaceful hairnet, my hands gloved with gentleness and my heart free of mold.

Studying His menu for purified lessons and blessin's around the lily pad,

Christina

"*If someone carries consecrated meat in the fold of their garment, and that fold touches some bread... or other food, does it become consecrated? The priests answered, 'No.' Then Haggai said, "If a person defiled by contact with a dead body touches one of these things, does it become defiled?' 'Yes,' the priests replied... Then Haggai said, 'So it is with this people and this nation in my sight,' declares the Lord. 'Whatever they do and whatever they offer there is defiled' " (Haggai 2:12-14).*

Cracked Up

I left a one-inch opening in my car window overnight, to air out the smell of my running shoes. Rainwater from an unexpected cloudburst found its way through that tiny air space and I opened my car door the following morning to find the driver's side soaked. Wet-dog stench replaced the running-shoe odor.

Instead of going back to the house to grab a towel, I used my jacket cuff to wipe the water from the dashboard and window. I drove with my fingertips until the steering wheel dried.

As I huddled toward the middle console, I realized how that little one-inch gap left miles worth of inconvenient discomfort. My back and left side were wet, I felt slimy, and I added a Shop-Vac and air freshener to my errand list.

While I suctioned the water from the car, I saturated in a FROG lesson. Satan only needs a small crack of an opening to access a deluge of destruction in our lives. The enemy wants to cause raging storms. And by chasing spiritual tornados, my misguided words and actions flow into a toxic cesspool.

Graciously, God only needs one tiny cry to save me from drowning in a polluted mind. He keeps me from becoming a victim of a flooded battlefield.

Jesus, thank you for being the weather stripping that bridges gaps. When I go through life's downpours, shelter me with Your seal of approval. Remind me You are the only One capable of walking on water.

Christina M. Eder

From the fresh waters of the lily pad,

Christina

"*...and do not give the devil a foothold*" (Ephesians 4:27).

Anticipate the Unknown

We traveled to Florida last week and, during a morning walk, Tig and I saw a frog perched atop a sign marker. We joked that I hadn't written a FROG Blog before we left Tennessee and maybe that frog was a reminder of my mission.

The next day, when we passed that same sign, I checked for the frog. I didn't see him (or her), but I did receive a FROG Blog lesson. God always shows up in new ways. Even though He is forever present, He creates assorted experiences to display His constant presence.

If I'm attentive, I can expect my Creator to show Himself through diversity. Sometimes, I see Him in nature, a conversation, billboard or song. Other times, I sense His presence through delays and seemingly ordinary encounters.

God's message of lavish love is steady. He uses unlimited treasures to teach His example of generosity. Like my writing, in which I strive to stream hope in its primary message. I package encouragement in various material to initiate vibrancy.

The universe was designed with routine, but within those respected cycles, we find unknowns (to us) to discover. By exploring new trails, I can awaken my senses to many different smells, sounds and views. With steady, focused movement, I keep myself from wearing a rut into life's path.

Jesus, thank You for Your creative examples of love. Guide me to view change as invigorating. Train me to accept fluctuations as part of Your transformation. Grow my courage to embrace joy in every surprise along the way.

Signing off, marked by a FROG moment,

Christina

"Instead of the thornbush will grow the juniper, and instead of briers the myrtle will grow" (Isaiah 55:13).

Voice Texts

When communication methods shifted toward electronic waves, I was saddened by my loss of personalized connection. And this sadness surprised me. As an introvert I require abundant quietness. I thrive in seclusion – but I wasn't accustomed to loneliness.

I socialize via snail mail, one-on-one walks or phone calls. People began responding to voice mails with texts. Sometimes within a minute of leaving a voice mail, the recipient texted, "Thanks for voice mail. Great to hear you." Based on their quick response, I figured the person was available to talk so I'd immediately call them back, only to be greeted again by their voice-mail message.

There's a three-hour time zone difference between our son and us. He and my husband exchange texts. I send cards and emails, but because of the time variance, there's been a disconnect in our personalized connection.

When we talk, we load up on updates, which sometimes leads to hour-long conversations. We often hang up with still more left to say. We're not fans of lengthy phone calls, so sometimes we can go weeks between verbal conversations.

Our son understands why I'm unable to text and we joke as soon as he handwrites a letter to me, I'll text him to say I've received it. To bridge our communication gap, we began "voice texting." We call each other Monday through Friday and leave brief voice messages. These include a funny story or memory, an inspirational quote, family news or a song.

He knows I flex my lunch break between 11:30-1:30 Eastern Time, so when he sees my number within that time, he knows I'm leaving a "verbal text." He leaves his "voice text" after work, while my phone is in its usual off mode.

These daily two-minute investments have yielded strong return. I'm grateful for this non-screen connection that has built our relationship.

Texting, LEFT VM

Christina

"Today, if you hear his voice, do not harden your hearts..." (Hebrews 3:15).

Joyfully Overweight

In a previous role, I worked at a nutritional center. During a weekly appointment, a client leaned toward me, almost conspiratorially, and whispered, "I know why my blood pressure and weight is higher this week. I'll tell you when we get back to your office."

The lady talked about how her family had unexpectedly asked if they could stay with her between their travels. She said, "I'm not your stereotypical mom or grandma. I love my family, but I dislike hosting overnight guests."

Thinking this lady was using backstory to divert discussion about her weight gain, I guided the conversation by saying, "Betty (not her actual name), I can imagine with your culinary skill, your guests appreciated your home cooking!"

She offered a knowing smile and said, "Of course, but after they left, I understood something bigger. Initially when my daughter called to ask if they could extend their visit, I felt the weight of my selfishness. I've gotten used to living alone and realized I'd need to reach for the heavy weights of patience and compassion."

She continued, "You've encouraged me to exercise with my diet so that lean muscle tone will develop. You also taught that muscle weighs more than fat. She winked. "After three days of housing two adults and young children, my stamina muscle must weigh a ton, don't you think?"

Joking aside, Betty said she exercised grace toward her guests. She believes the scale indicated her heart gained at least two and a half pounds of love and patience for her family.

This lady's hospitality taught me that though her creature comforts were temporarily compromised, she found value in relaxing her routine. She replaced her stringent repetition with a welcoming floor mat exercise.

Lifting weights of encouragement,

Christina

"Offer hospitality to one another without grumbling" (1 Peter 4:9).

Beware!

Danger. 911. Warning. Emergency. These alerts cause me to stop and pay attention. I need to discover the source of alarm. Sometimes I need to act. Other times, someone else is required to assist. And sometimes the best resolution is to wait and let the storm run its course.

Ouch! Stop! Slam! No! These harsh sounds also implore me to halt. Based on memories, I always associate these noises with distress or injury. I've experienced physical bumps and scars, but perhaps my most intense bruises have hit my heart or crushed my spirit.

Healthcare workers and emergency-response professionals dedicate their life's work to serving the injured. Their best efforts are not beyond their expertise, but sometimes the outcome of the situation is out of their hands.

Only Jesus can continuously heal someone or something. His proven resume includes curing anxiety and treating bitterness. He's able to stitch forgiveness, diagnose resentment and keep the soul alive before it dies of hypothermia.

In the same way an audible signal grabs my attention, I can cry out to Jesus to protect every part of me, including my heart, mind and spirit.

My Physician and Healer, thank You for being on call 24/7 with Your perfect solutions. Help me answer Your calls and instruct me to remain calm while You handle my pleas.

Christina M. Eder

Remind me to frequently thank You for learning Your help is on its way.
On the stretcher of life,

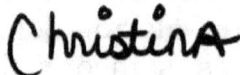

"The lion has roared – who will not fear? The Sovereign Lord has spoken – who can but prophesy?" (Amos 3:8).

Tempered

Gross! Yuck!

I grabbed a glass of milk on the counter, thinking my husband had just poured it for me to welcome me home. Anticipating a cold, refreshing drink, I shuddered when I slurped a mouthful of room-temperature milk.

I quickly realized Tig had poured a glass of milk for himself at breakfast and forgotten to drink it before he left for work.

I had expected refreshment. Even on that 80-degree day, I would have preferred hot water over tepid milk. Its indifferent temperature reminded me I pour so much energy into a day and sometimes allow myself to overfill hours. That leaves me only enough to half-heartedly serve God. I ladle Him a spiritual cup of cold, watery broth instead of a bowl of hot, thick, hearty stew.

When God spoke through Amos, He said He was ready to spit the lukewarm people out of His mouth. That swallow of warmish milk helped me relate to God's not wanting or even deserving my misplaced or lackluster efforts.

Jesus, You went to the cross with heated passion. Though the world turned a cold shoulder to You, You responded with a loving fire. Ignite my awareness to guard our relationship. Align my priorities to prevent me from becoming dying embers. Blaze my desire to fill others' cups with Your kindness.

From cold to hot, insulating myself against lukewarm living,

Christina M. Eder

"I know your deeds, that you are neither cold nor hot. I wish you were either one or the other! So, because you are lukewarm – neither hot or cold – I am about to spit you out of my mouth" (Revelation 3:15-16).

Jesus: From Introvert to Extrovert

I read this Scripture and relate to Jesus' preference in social settings. I also prefer to attend gatherings as a quietly engaged observer.

In a culture that overstimulates me, I find great value in listening-to-understand one person at a time. I see a trend that dishonors individuality. Many people talk, yet few seem to listen without interruption. I appreciate when someone's experience interlocks with mine, but I've found that by interjecting my relatability, I devalue that speaker's story.

According to the Bible, Jesus used minimal dialogue. In Mark 7:24, when He entered this home, Jesus didn't want His presence acknowledged. However, God had other plans. He hadn't sent His Son to fly under the radar. People needed to learn who God was through Jesus in human form.

People knew Jesus was their assurance that in God's care, He supplied everlasting provision. Jesus, as human, wanted quiet appearances; however, God magnified Himself by surrounding His Son with others.

Jesus could have healed everyone in one fell swoop, yet He often chose single house calls to complete His mission. He changed the entire world through these small singular interactions.

With God's foundation, Jesus stepped down from heaven to lift others up. Even when He may have felt outcast or yearned to retreat, He allowed God to eternally use Him.

We have quick (even instant) access to endless connection, yet there's a growing epidemic that people are lonely-in-the-crowd. I see faces seeking a personal touch, a smile, eye contact or an understanding ear.

Lord, help me become more like Jesus. I seek to use His example of responding to others' needs with immediate obedience. Lead me to encourage and engage individuals one story at a time.

Stepping out from shadows of the lily pad,

Christina

"...He entered a house and did not want anyone to know it; yet he could not keep his presence secret" (Mark 7:24).

Off the Grid or Sheltered?

A fellow author was asked whether she feels distanced from the world, as much of her writing career includes solitude. This woman said she prefers to consider her solitary lifestyle as being sheltered, not inaccessible.

She believes any news or people she needs to address will show up, provided she remains aware and available. Though she recognizes the value of having access to endless communication, she has discovered peace by embracing life on a need-to-know basis.

In Samuel 17, Absalom is on a hunt to kill David, his father. He plans his attack for when David is weak, because he has seen his father's success as a warrior. Hushai, David's confidant, reminds Absalom David will battle as necessary, whether he's hidden in a cave or exposed in a city.

God promises a shield for His people. He isn't stymied by isolation or elevation. God's fierce love and protection for His believers is like a mama bear standing at her cave entry, ready to defend her cubs from any predators that pose a threat to their safety.

When it's God's time, He leads me out of a sheltered cave, often to exercise my trust in Him. He brings me, His human cub, outdoors so I can adjust my eyes to new light.

I may be attacked in seclusion or out in public, but I've experienced God's spotless record of victory. His heart is a lion; His mercy is a lamb. I'm never separated from my Fearless Warrior because I'm sheltered and protected by His armor.

Bravely stepping onto a protected lily pad of FROG Blog living,

Christina

"Then even the bravest soldier, whose heart is like the heart of a lion, will melt with fear, for all Israel knows that your father is a fighter and that those with him are brave" (2 Samuel 17:10).

A Great Day. Really?

We're going to have a great day! We enjoyed a great meal! Great days and great food. That sounds, well... great!

I associate the word "great" with positive memories and laughworthy moments.

Zephaniah 1:14 writes about the great day of the Lord. When I initially read this verse, I got excited. "Okay, Lord, let's see this great day. I can't wait!" My anticipation builds when Zephaniah continues, "It's near and coming quickly." I envision "quick" in terms of hours or maybe weeks. I want to see this rapidly approaching great day!

I read on... "The cry on the day of the Lord is bitter."

Thud!

Wait. Is he still talking about the same great day? In Zephaniah's explanation, great means powerful and mighty. He writes that the great day includes enormous distress, excessive ruin, unlimited blackness and boundless gloom. All mighty.

Not powerfully sounding so great.

Zephaniah's saga continues. There will be blood and no amount of gold or silver will protect against the Lord's fiery finish. That doesn't sound like a happy ending.

Until God intervenes.

Scripture says a remnant of believers will be spared; God will care for them and restore their fortunes. This teaching shows me how gracious God is to foreshadow a warning. His loving invitation is intended to encourage me to engage my free will to believe and follow.

This great day forecast isn't meant to frighten, but to protect me when I pursue what the Lord considers great (joy, peace, unity, wisdom and truth, to name a few). When I show up for life to love my Creator and His creations, I can associate the great day with a victory cry.

Until the great day, I'm pursuing greatness for this day on the lily pad of life,

Christina

"*The Great day of the Lord is near-near and coming quickly...*" *(Zephaniah 1:14-16).*

Breaking to Decipher

I'm preparing for next week's solo silent retreat. I'm investing that time to develop my word for this year. Decipher.

In my "new lease on life" vision, I've chosen to ask myself, "What is my motive?"

My deciphering practice includes all facets of my life. Money and time; relationships and community outreach; writing projects and life-coaching opportunities. What is my genuine desire behind every yes or no?

In visualizing the *Survivor* show, I have voted once-important priorities and some contestants off my Emerald Isle. I've shifted my survivor mentality into a greener outlook.

In Emily P. Freeman's podcast, "The Next Right Thing," she teaches that abundant possibilities can frequently lead to decision fatigue. Her insight helped me question whether I'm being mindful or simply mind full.

When I find myself facing multiple choices, I've learned to incorporate a method of deciphering by allowing myself two or three options. Unless it's a life-threatening decision, I encourage myself to choose quickly. (I can easily practice deciphering at any American store where whole aisles are dedicated solely to breakfast cereals and hair products.)

I've asked the Holy Spirit to grant me discernment when He answers, "Go," "No," "Slow" or "Whoa." Go and no are clear cut. My challenge is in understanding God's slow and whoa answers.

To me, slow means, "yes, but proceed with methodical caution." Whoa speaks to my inner mustang when I try to outrun my reins. That deciphering spirit graciously lassoes me back into the rodeo circle.

As I pack for my retreat I'm traveling light and staying at a primitive cottage with limited options but ample comfort. I anticipate I'll survive *and* flourish through simplicity.

One decision, two options, a trinity of abundance.

Deciphering from the lily pad on new freedom island,

Christina

"There is a way that appears to be right, but in the end, it leads to death" (Proverbs 14:12).

Time's Up

Time's up. There it went. Time got away. I just lived another end-of-times moment. Another. And another.

There's been increased talk about end times. I hear people saying how we're living in the last days. In groups, leaders encourage their listeners to be prepared. Jesus is coming back soon.

From my newly realized vantage point, this worldly view is theoretically accurate. We live the end of times each second. That second is an end. That minute becomes the final one. That hour will never begin again. Scientifically, we're correct in saying we're living in a world that is ending.

As Matthew wrote in his gospel, not even Jesus knew when the end of times would happen. In Matthew 24, Jesus listed signs that will indicate the world's deadline. Even Jesus, as His Father's Son, didn't know the year, day or hour. In reading that even Jesus didn't know when His Dad would end the world, I surprisingly gained freedom from concern.

When I first heard that we need to be prepared, I worried I wasn't ready. That worry led to not comprehending what prepared fully meant. With the idea that every second is the end, it's lessened my angst about when or if today is the end of times.

My focus shifted to be attentive to each hour, the end of a day, the end of a conversation. Would I spend my last hour this way? How did I invest my last words? What will I seek to learn at the end of this day?

Finalizing this reflective pondering with a leap into a new ending,

Christina

"Heaven and earth will pass away, but my words will never pass away. But about that day or hour, no one knows, not even the angels in heaven, nor the Son, but only the Father" (Matthew 24:35-36).

Change of Venue

I began a new writing project and needed a perspective shift. I do my best writing in sunlight, often perched in the open hatch of my car. Our housing complex has no assigned parking and residents often choose their "usual spot." I changed my typical parking space so my open hatch faced direct light.

My neighbors have grown accustomed to seeing me in my vehicular office. They've previously stopped to ask if I'm okay or find out why I'm sitting in the open hatch. One neighbor nicknamed me "The Trunk Writer."

Yesterday, I parked further from my building, which led passing neighbors to look twice as they drove. Some stopped to question my relocation. After several such inquiries, I realized how one simple change of my routine caused people to pause.

In Paul's letter to Timothy, he cautioned him to be diligent in using his gifts. I try to be diligent about siting in a certain place, during a set time every day, to use my writing gifts. I find it fascinating how one slight adjustment to accommodate lighting needs could prompt people to take such notice. I've heard when we look for something, we search for what stands out from a customary routine.

That experience showed me how subtle shifts in location can invite updated perspectives and responses. I wonder how much one altered thought, attitude, comment or action can generate change.

Does a conversation inspire or weary? Does an interaction encourage or dishearten? I want to be diligent in using my gifts to uplift downtrodden areas, one slight movement at a time.

Pausing to consider inner adaptation on a lily pad of learning,

Christina

"*Be diligent in these matters; give yourself wholly to them, so that everyone will see your progress*" (1 Timothy 4:15).

Working on Fallow Ground

Several years ago, I stopped making online purchases or going to stores on Sunday. I believe if I'm to honor God's weekly vacation day, it's selfish of me to expect others to serve my whims. Barring life-threatening emergencies, I don't want to impose on anyone's keeping holy the Sabbath Day.

I heard a DJ say she wishes every week had one day to complete her need-to-do list, one day for her want-to-do and one day for nothing on her calendar. Her comment inspired me to divide my weekend into those three segments. In visualizing my weekend to include two thirds of want-to-do and nothing-to-do, I'm more determined to tackle the need-to-do tasks.

Those three elements may not be equally divided, but anticipating play and rest in every weekend makes essential chores reasonable. There's a similarity between want-to-dos and need-to-dos. At the end of a day or weekend, both will be incomplete. Rarely do I hear people talk about completing everything from their want-to activities.

God instructed farmers to give the land and animals a break on the seventh day. In Deuteronomy, Hebrew Law required all debts to be removed after seven years (Deuteronomy 15:1). God set His example of blending work and rest into His seven days of Creation.

He used six days to design our world and the last day to reflect on His progress. Everything is perpetually being shaped or taking shape. Like my plans, God's work and playful evolution is never finished, either. If God can craft the universe and still take a day off, I will learn to follow His lead.

Soaking and serving from the lily pad of life,

Christina

"At the end of every seven years you must cancel debts" (Deuteronomy 15:1).

Growing Potential

"I don't measure America by its achievement, but by its potential." (Shirley Chisholm, *Country Magazine*, July 2020).

Country Magazine photographed a toddler driver with a puppy in his truck bed. This young chauffeur delivers an adult-sized grin behind the steering wheel of his Little Tikes truck. His noble expression implies, "I have precious K-9 cargo to haul."

He isn't concerned that his truck is plastic. He's enthused about accomplishing his mission.

I've watched teary moms and proud dads cheering kindergartners at graduation. Grandparents temporarily disregard arthritic pain while they click their cameras. It's hard to hear someone tell any student, "Good start, but you've got a long way before your high-school diploma." Or, "That's just a drop in your bucket. You're oceans away from a college degree." (Regretfully, I've made my own parenting comment doozies.)

It's degrading to hear these statements at any event, yet sometimes I still tell myself, "Sure, you took that step, but there's hundreds of steps until..."

Until what? Comfort? Approval? Completion? Then what?

Learning isn't designed to stop. I love being a student in earth's classroom. Sometimes I'm like a distracted kindergartner with a crayon bucket and given only a dozen of them to for ten minutes. I want more colors. More time. More paper. My Teacher gives me only what He knows I can handle within that moment.

Jesus invites children. I've never read about Jesus telling the little children to grow up. He heals lepers. He doesn't distance himself until the leper is clean. He meets people on their learning ladder and climbs with them.

Some people are in elementary stages of development. Others are well-schooled in their skill. We are called to be teachers and learners. Like Little Tikes drivers, we move toward our potential.

Class dismissed on the lily pad of life,

Christina

"If you know his will and approve of what is superior because you are instructed by the law; if you are convinced that you are a guide for the blind, a light for those who are in the dark, an instructor of the foolish, a teacher of little children, because you have I the law the embodiment of knowledge and truth-you, then who teach others, do you not teach yourself? You who preach against stealing, do you steal?" (Romans 12:18-21).

A Pigheaded Lesson

"Little pig, little pig, let me in!"

"Not by the hair of my chinny-chin-chin."

"Then I'll huff and I'll puff and I'll blow your house in!"

This conversation between pigs and a wolf blows me away with three lessons to build upon.

Three pigs. One mission. Construct a house. Pig #1 quickly erects a house of straw. The wolf, posing as a home inspector, blows the doors off Pig #1's home.

While the wolf licks his chops, Pig #2 labors over his wooden abode. Mr. Wolf uses his signature huff-and-puff assessment and soon Pig #2's house goes up in smoke. I suspect the wolf used that house's kindling to fire up the grill for a rib dinner.

Considering how the wolf tested architecture, Pig #3 chose a brick-and-mortar option. The final inspection came, but this time the wolf wasted his breath. No amount of hot air could destroy those bricks. I imagine Pig #3 looking out his window at the defeated wolf and hollering, "Hogwash!"

Matthew 7:24-27 teaches about building my life on rocks. Rocks of value. Stones of perseverance. Pebbles of trust. Sometimes my courage resembles a straw house and doubt appears to be a stack of twigs.

We're all architects, designing blueprints into our life practice. Jesus establishes His building codes, to protect us when the wolves come knocking on our door. I need to remember I am protected under His code if I build according to His standards. If so, when I lay a brick of truth into my foundation, I'm assured of God's shelter. I may witness the effects of windstorms, but I breathe a sigh of relief in knowing God defends me.

With a determined huff and a rekindled puff, I leap with wind in my sails,

Christina

"Therefore everyone who hears these words of mine and puts them into practice is like a wise man who built his house on the rock. The rain came down, the streams rose, and the winds blew and beat against that house; yet it did not fall, because it had its foundation on the rock" (Matthew 7:24-25).

Audio Delusion

"Give me a laser gun down the road that I must travel. Gimme a laser..."

I sang these words to a popular '80s song by Mr. Mister. The tune had received much airtime, so I often practiced my inner rock-star routine.

Years later, that song came on when I was transporting a youth group. The kids joined me as I belted out, "Give me a laser gun..." The crowd grew quiet and I heard whispered snickers.

A student spoke up, "Miss Christina, what did just you sing?"

Thinking he wanted an encore I sang the refrain.

One brave soul said, "That doesn't even make sense."

I defended my interpretation and how lasers point us in the right direction. I explained virtual light sabers defend us down the road that we must travel.

A young man shook his head and said, "Hate to break it to ya, but your old song is called *Kyrie Eleison*."

Later, I learned "Kyrie Eleison" means, "Lord have mercy" in Latin.

Three decades (and frequent story royalties later), I'm enlightened with a musical learning note. I'm aware of optical illusions and subjected to audio delusions. I hear one thing and construe another meaning.

In Matthew's gospel, after Jesus' crucifixion, the Pharisees approached Pilate and recounted how "that deceiver" said He'd rise again. They translated His words into their logical terms.

They seal proofed the tomb. They feared if Jesus' words played out, His disciples would broadcast that He rose from the dead. They worried this deception would be worse than Jesus' original proclamation.

I recognize the real words to "Give me a Laser Gun" after someone armed me with the truth. Jesus plays His Greatest Hits collection that includes a Resurrection song. Lord, have mercy over my soul.

Tuning in from the Martha & Mary Writing Studio,

Christina

(Tune in next week when I sing my dad's version of Billy Idol's interpretation of Eyes Without a Face! ☺)

"...we remember that while he was still alive that deceiver said, "After three days I will rise again. So give the order for the tomb to be made secure until the third day. Otherwise, his disciples may come and steal the body and tell the people that he has been raised from the dead. This last deception will be worse than the first" (Matthew 27:63-64).

When I'm 18!

"I can't wait until I'm 18!"

"When I have a house, I won't..."

"The first thing I'll do when I move out is..."

I heard these phrases when our son was growing up. He used the same lines and logic I had practiced on my parents. It's tough when I realize the apple doesn't fall far from the tree.

During thorny patches, when he would retort, "I can't wait until I'm 18 so I can move out," my inner child agreed.

I wanted to respond, "Finally! We share the same viewpoint right now!"

In Genesis 3, I read about Adam and Eve's testing God with their rebellious attitudes. Their Father loved them unconditionally. He provided everything. God had created perfect living conditions, and yet they sought what they believed to be greener pastures.

God offered a nearly endless buffet for His children. They indulged in the one off-limits tree and ate themselves out of house and home. They traded God's inherently wealthy lifestyle for a lifetime of pain.

I relate to Adam and Eve. I sometimes pack my suitcase with personal agendas, possessions and relationships and set out to find better plans than what God crafted. He has allowed me to deceive myself in believing I was becoming a self-made woman, created in my image and likeness.

Fortunately, even when I've moved from my Father's house, He didn't change the locks. He didn't change His address. I knocked on

His door, seeking parental advice, and He allowed me to permanently move back in.

Instead of thinking something else looks more marketable, I can see the fruits of God's labor. Now I anticipate living every day under God's roof. I can't wait until I'm 51, 52, 53, 54...

Moving toward an eternal garden (that doesn't have house insurance, taxes, expiration dates or weeds),

Christina

"So the Lord banished him from the Garden of Eden to work the ground from which he had been taken (Genesis 3:23).

Merciful Attire

Food, shelter and clothing. I've learned these are essential for survival. Gratefully, I have all three of these, plus some minimal luxuries.

Sometimes when I dread a grocery visit or house chores, I think of people who have little to no food.

For some, home is a downtown warming shelter, a car or a street. And as much as I dislike shopping, especially for clothes, I'd be hard pressed if I had an empty closet.

Genesis 3:21 offers a peek at Adam and Eve's wardrobe. God made them garments of skin. None of my fashion designs conjure runway model images; however, I do see a window display of God's grace. His wayward kids sold out during their Tree of Life experience. They pawned their naked freedom for clearance-rack duds. Even though they disobeyed God's one instruction, He made them clothes before they made their journey out of Eden.

God's original design was stain-proof. Instead of discontinuing His altered pattern, He sent all generations following Adam and Eve out with everything we need for our trek back to His eternal Garden of Eden.

I see these skin garments as representation that our flesh is exposed to elements of a fallen world. Humorously, I wonder if Adam and Eve's clothes became the first "skinny" jeans.

When I'm tempted to fuss about what I do or don't have, I remember God's daily food, shelter, clothing and love. He clothes me with protection and dresses me with kindness.

Walking on the runway toward red carpet Light,

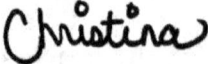

"*The Lord God made garments of skin for Adam and his wife and clothed them (Genesis 3:21).*

TADPOLES: Tiny Tales from Freshwater Adventures

Recall Notice

I remember when one of my Frog Blog books was published with a grainy cover and muddy-print back. The layout was the best to date but the exterior left a lasting impression (although sometimes lasting impressions aren't exactly favorable).

Short jaunt through time-consuming details... the cover received a facelift, but during its reset, I felt like the situation would end my established credibility. This week, news stories also reminded me I'm not a solo driver on life's switchbacks.

A car manufacturer needed to recall thousands of vehicles with faulty wiring. One acclaimed soup company accidentally mislabeled meatball stew as organic chicken noodle soup. A surgeon was being sued for operating on a patient's healthy knee. All jobs have reconstruction stories in their book of business.

Thankfully, my resolution to readers who received shady-covered books didn't involve injury or lawsuit. I wish everyone would have responded with Jesus' example from Luke 6:37. "Do not judge and you will not be judged. Do not condemn, and you will not be condemned. Forgive and you will be forgiven."

I had many supportive people during my literary recall. They remembered what they had learned from others during their own misguided experiences. I appreciate the encouragers who reminded me, in various ways, sin is a mistake, but a mistake is not necessarily sin. My motive wasn't malicious, "just" inconvenient.

To car manufacturers, soup companies, surgeons, authors and everybody with roundabout street cred, I invite all of us to drive compassion into our motives. When we are tenderhearted, we lessen the road rage that can go in a direction of misunderstanding.

Remembering mile markers in my lessons and blessin's from life on a lily pad,

Christina

"Remember the days of old; consider the generations long past. Ask your father and he will tell you, your elders, and they will explain to you (Deuteronomy 32:7).

Incomplete Education

I graduated with a business administration degree 30 years prior to entering my vocation. I left three decades of jobs to answer God's ad to tutor aspiring authors and write.

The first three years resembled my college days. This hungry student fought with intensity. In various corporate venues, I worked with integrity, but my heart didn't fit within a company's flow chart.

I committed to writing and tutoring with 40 years of freelance writing and job-related assignments. I didn't consider myself a "real" author, though.

My first year out, I anticipated small projects for income while I prepared to publish two books. Instead, I encountered companies who "borrowed" what they had "hired" me to write. (Most people consider this practice stealing) That year resembled freshman year at a Literary Learning Center.

The second year, I established a social-media presence, published my first two books and took on tutoring clients. With books to sell and a third one finished, I bought into the trend that social media was the marketplace's golden calf. I figured, through online exposure, I'd recoup my publishing and business startup expenses. (Thank God for a savings account!)

In my third year, I had that third book published and my fourth one finished. People promised to create podcasts and videos for me. Their pledges didn't come to fruition and I adopted a bitter taste. I didn't trust anyone's word, including God's. I finally went (back) to my Guidance Counselor and He realigned me with wisdom. I left His office recharged.

I graduate with the understanding my education is incomplete. I will be a lifetime student earning my street cred. I declare my major: literary pastor for the Lord. Graduation will be determined by my Headmaster.

Fishing on the continuing-ed. lily pad and learning from online lessons,

Christina

"As long as it is day, we must do the works of him who sent me..."*(John 9:4).*

Addressing My Distractions

A friend noticed I had a different journal than when we previously visited. She asked about my journaling practice and I explained how I need to write my happenings and requests to focus on what God teaches me.

I explained through reviewing journals, I learn about who God is because I see what He has done. Sometimes I'm grateful for what He *hasn't* done.

She wondered when and how I learned to pray. I told her I've tried as many spiritual techniques as some people try in weight-loss and fitness programs. And in the process, I've found each practice works different muscles.

She was overwhelmed by numerous resources. She said she gets easily distracted when she seeks quiet and only finds herself thinking about her tasks.

I reassured her I experience similar challenges. I cued her in to my most basic centering strategy. Her eyes lit up, and I could tell her curiosity was piqued. I said I carry a printed list of my contacts in my car. When my mind moves away (sometimes without a forwarding address), I take those contact sheets, speak the person's name, picture their face and ask God to light, guard, rule and guide their day.

Now she looked disappointedly amused. "That's *it?*"

We laughed at the simplicity but when I'm in a whirlwind, that's how I ground myself to chat briefly with my Creator. There's a time for devotionals, Bible study and reflection, but sometimes I need quick fundamentals to recollect my scattered thoughts.

In Matthew 6:9-14, Jesus teaches His disciples how to pray. He instructs them, "do not keep on babbling like pagans, for they think they will be heard because of their many words" (Matthew 6:7).

If Jesus recommends a few faithful words, I will address Him accordingly.

Signed, sealed, delivered with confirmation from the lily pad,

Christina

"Our Father in heaven, hallowed be your name... and lead us not into temptation, but deliver us from the evil one" (Matthew 6:9-14).

Well, I'll Be!

Job applications request character references. Often, potential employers want at least three people to fill them in about what their candidates offer.

I've given job references and employers consistently value an applicant's honesty and attendance. They ask about customer spirit and teammate interaction. Rarely am I asked about someone's software proficiency, computer skills or certified education. Qualifications and education can lead to an interview. An interview determines employment. The crux of a hiring decision appears to surround who the person is.

In Titus 1:6, Paul provides a job description for town elders. "An elder must be blameless. He must not be open to being wild and disobedient. He needs to be hospitable."

Paul's background check involves the prospective candidate's character. He cares about who the person *is* before he considers what they *do*.

People act in accordance with who they are. Employers have said they can train nearly anyone, as long as the employee consistently shows up with a willingness to learn and then follows through with eager kindness.

When the Jewish people disputed who Jesus was, He responded, "I AM" (John 8:21-58).

He invites me to a covenant with Him, first based on who He is. In His faithfulness, He seals me with love, and I respond, "I do because of Who You are."

Accepting God's proposal to join His team on the FROG Blog,

Christina

"An elder must be blameless... not open to the charge of being wild and disobedient. ... he must be hospitable, one who loves what is good, who is self-controlled, upright, holy and disciplined" (Titus 1:6-8).

What Can I Do Other Than...?

My husband and I hit a spell where we had multiple deaths in a six-month stretch. Based on these circumstances, we attended more funerals and fewer baby showers.

That stretch left our muscles weakened as the endurance tests required intensity. We have learned when we face life's inclines, we find it best to express our concerns with God and each other. Period.

Sometimes after our situational marathon has run its course, we give a few details to close friends. We prefer to focus on how we learned from the situation, not what we experienced. In extreme circumstances, we reach out to one or two confidential prayer warriors during the climb.

Tig and I have discovered kind-hearted people offer well-intentioned advice and want to fix or solve. We engage in a less-is-more philosophy, especially during volatile circumstances. Less talking. Fewer attempts to force a solution. Less publicity.

We firmly believe if a thought is big enough to think about, it's big enough to pray about.

When friends ask what they can do, we request trustworthy prayers.

Some respond, "But what can I do besides pray?" Or "What can I do other than talk to God?"

In situations like this, I prefer to ask, "In addition to prayer, how can I support you?" It's been a subtle shift in questioning, but I've seen a tremendous difference in answers.

We've come to a place, through trial and much error, where we see value in spiritual growth over physical impressions. Everything matters to God and our priority as husband and wife is to repair and fix our spirit.

Speaking from filtered waters around the lily pad,

Christina

"What good is it for someone to gain the whole world, yet forfeit their soul? Or what can anyone give in exchange for their soul?" (Mark 8:36-37).

Blocked Out

I was interviewed about my writing career and how an author's lifestyle appears intriguing to some people. A common question circles around writer's block.

I shared this strategy. Sometimes a barrier is self-imposed. When I dread a potentially volatile call, the dust behind a door suddenly becomes a priority. If I am to write a proposal, non-emergency emails get an immediate reply. I'd rather make a dentist appointment than make some decisions.

To redirect my mind, I write. Actually, I copy something already written. As soon as I catch myself taking a detour, I can lessen further delay by handwriting a quote, poem, Scripture or a book excerpt.

I allow myself a three-minute pit stop. This written rerouting is not meant to become a new rabbit trail to follow.

Our Creator gave us complex minds with a capacity to handle many moving pieces. We're prone to wander and it takes practice to keep a steady pace. My Manufacturer installed a navigation system to guide me on the highway of life. It's up to me to connect the dots on God's map.

Merging my thoughts, activities and priorities into today's traffic around the lily pad,

Christina

"...but to see another law at work in me, waging war against the law of my mind and making me a prisoner of the law of sin at work within me" (Romans 7:23).

Christina M. Eder

Leggo My Eggo!

"Leggo my Eggo!" is a commercialized tagline to market waffles. It features two people sitting by a toaster waiting for their waffle. They both reach for the waffle as it pops up. With one hand on the waffle and both eyes on the other person, one of the hungry contestants yields. Then the smiling waffle winner chomps into a victory bite.

Mom's homemade waffles cooked any competition, but we always clamored for Eggo waffles so we could reenact this commercial.

I later babysat for a family who bought Eggos, and one morning while I made breakfast, the child asked to help.

The youngster was learning to read, so I asked him to go around the kitchen to identify words. He recognized salt and learned what j-u-i-c-e spelled. He looked at the waffle box, sounded out E-g-g-o and excitedly reported, "This spells ego!"

I explained Eggo was a brand name pronounced Egg-o, not ego.

What if a reminder popped up when I needed to leggo my ego? It might not sell waffles, but this commercial served me a lesson about humility.

My ego shows up through expectations and timeframes. What if I released my ego? What would happen if I freed my ego and surrendered it to Someone Else? By compromising, I worry I'm giving up. Will I become a pushover? Will I be judged as passive?

God teaches me about authentic humility through Jesus' example on earth. Jesus is meek but not timid. Gentle, not complacent. An apathetic person wouldn't surrender ego to accept crucifixion. Jesus faced a humiliating death in the public eye. In God's eyes, He became triumphant.

I take my hand off the toaster as if to say, "Lord take my ego so I can serve you first."

Humbly waffling between control and surrender on the lily pad,

Christina

"All of you, clothe yourselves with humility toward one another, because God opposes the proud but shows favor to the humble" (1 Peter 5:5).

Christina M. Eder

The Best Relationship
Katie D.

When I think about relationships, the first one that jumps to my mind is my relationship with God. This relationship has always been special to me because I know He will never leave my side. He is always there for me and doesn't stop loving me when I make a mistake. He always forgives me; all I have to do is ask.

When I look for someone to talk to, He is always listening. I always have a wonderful friend right here by my side when I need one. It is amazing, knowing someone cares for me and always will, and that He is the Creator of everything. I have friends in my neighborhood and we sometimes get into fights, but I never have to worry about that with God. He is always there, no matter what.

Everything He does for all of us He does out of His grace. It is definitely not because we deserve it. Even if we don't think we need Him in our lives, it would be much harder to go through life without Jesus Christ, our Lord and Savior. If you want to have a stronger relationship with God, like the one I'm describing, all you have to do is ask Him into your heart.

Katie D. is a rising fifth grader in Knoxville, Tennessee. The middle child of a middle child, Katie has always placed great value on relationships in life. She accepted Christ and was baptized in 2016, and her relationship with God shapes everything in the rest of her life. In her spare time, Katie enjoys reading and writing, and is a competitive swimmer.

Christina M. Eder

A Changing Leaf
Irelyn

My first year of middle school was a drastic change from what I was used to in elementary school. I was scared and felt so alone, crying myself to sleep every night. But God wasn't going to abandon me in my despair. He responded in the most surprising way.

One morning as I was walking toward the school building, I was struck by an image of a patched brown-and-white cat with luminous green eyes. He sat near the school doors, watching me. I instantly knew I wasn't just imagining the cat, though no one else seemed to notice him.

He followed me inside, and immediately I felt calmer. Throughout my day the cat accompanied me everywhere, even perching on my shoulder during band class. I decided to name him Leaf.

My mom could see a difference in me when she picked me up from school that day. I told her about my experience, and she asked me who I thought the cat was. I didn't hesitate when I responded, "Jesus."

Whether the cat was Jesus himself or perhaps some sort of angel, I didn't know, but there was no doubt in my mind that Leaf was a gift from God.

The days passed and Leaf stayed by my side. However, after Christmas break, I returned to school and quickly noticed I didn't see Leaf anywhere. I panicked for a moment but was relieved to find him sitting on top of my locker.

This time when Leaf looked down at me, I recognized a new meaning in his beautiful green eyes. It was a farewell. I suddenly realized I wasn't scared anymore, and I didn't need Leaf. It was time to let him go. I smiled sadly and told my feline friend goodbye, and I haven't seen him since.

The lesson I've learned from my encounter with Leaf is even if I feel like there is no escape from the darkness around me, have faith. God is with me. Who knows? Maybe he'll even send a little feline miracle to guide you out!

Thirteen-year-old Irelyn is a prolific writer, avid reader and adorer of cats. She published her first book, Call of the Free, *at the age of 10 and has been creating new stories ever since. When she's not reading or writing, you can find her playing soccer, performing in local theaters or messing around with her friends and family.*

Christina M. Eder

The Healing Power of the Outdoors
Ben

I find fishing is one of my favorite pastimes. It allows me to sit back and relax and think about life. It doesn't matter if I am standing on the bank or sitting in a boat.

There is something about being in nature that you can't find anywhere else. The waves hitting the boat and the shore and being outside. It lets me reflect on life and allows me to step back from the busyness of life and slow down and look at the path on which life is taking me. It clears my mind and allows me to think better. It may not work for everyone, but if it does, you won't regret it.

Another thing that allows me to think is just being alone. You should take time out of your day to reflect about the choices you made and the person you want to be. If you have a goal you should ask yourself, "What did I do today to help me get closer to that achievement?" If you find you haven't done anything, think of something small, even if it is a reminder to do something.

Ben is a high school sophomore from Wisconsin. He is not a big fan of school but loves the outdoors and fishing. He even creates his own lures.

Making Connections Through Music
Josie E.

I find myself to be most alive when I'm listening to music, because the lyrics connect to me. I'm not talking about just the regular connection with everyday things, I'm talking about connection that links to my own soul. Whenever I have a bad day or something even worse has happened, I can turn on music and it seems to stitch me back together.

Music brings my spirit up and lets me sort through things in my life that are tangled together and need untangling. Some songs make me feel like I can conquer the world and take up the responsibility of anything and everything at once.

When new songs come out, I can listen to the words and find connection in them. It lights me up in a way that's non-explainable, because I found that one thing that makes sense to me.

The thing about music that really gets me is that the artists of music aren't thinking of me specifically. They think about what relates to everyone, but when that song still manages to relate to me, it's amazing. When a song comes out and I just automatically vibe to it, it makes me wonder if this connection the artists have can tell what everyone needs at that moment.

I'm a traveling and changing spirit. I want to be everywhere and nowhere at the same time. I constantly feel like I'm chained against the wall and can't decide what's best for me and what I need to survive. The stress of school, global pandemic and work makes it seem like heavier and heavier chains are being put on me, threatening to bring me down.

Christina M. Eder

When I listen to that one song that connects me in a way that no one else can, it makes me dream of a world that can be better. That dream, that hope, is what keeps me tethered to this world.

Josie is a high-school freshman from Wisconsin. She is a lover of music, the outdoors, reading, art and all animals.

These Are a Few of My Favorite Things
Connor

An experience that has helped me understand life in a different way was when one day I thought of homeless people and thought of how their life is an everyday struggle. This became important because it taught me to be grateful for what I have.

The person who has taught me most about discipline is my dad because he always talks to my brother and me whenever we start getting in trouble.

My favorite place to go to motivate me is in my room with one of my pets. Pets keep me calm. I like to pet their fur because it's soft and fluffy, which makes me feel calm. Sometimes they sleep on my lap or right next to me.

I have a guinea pig named Buckbeak. I have a cat named Clover and three dogs: Libby, Cricket and Thunder.

I have 11 fish, but we could not think of enough names and how to tell one from another. I got two of the fish when I was in kindergarten and they had babies a year ago. We got our rabbit, Buttercup, for my Dad for Father's Day. Our hamster is Phoenix.

One of my favorite things about Christ is how He saves us from evil. Another amazing thing is how God sent His only son to take on our punishment. When I was baptized, I was relieved because I had been looking forward to that moment for about half a year. One of my favorite Bible stories is when three men got thrown into a furnace by King Nebuchadnezzar and they came out alive. It inspired me on how God can do things like that.

Christina M. Eder

    I like to play cello because it brings a variety to my life and I have fun playing it. I enjoy the part where we have to cooperate together to perform a song in orchestra.
    Hiking gives me a chance to enjoy wildlife while getting a workout in for the day. It's also fun with a buddy, because you have someone to talk to. I hike in the Great Smoky Mountain National Park. I like trails that are eight to 12 miles long with a high elevation. I usually hike with my grandmother and brother or my grandfather and brother.

I'm Connor, an 11-year-old boy who lives in Maryville, Tennessee. I got to share my favorite things in my story.

God is Mysterious in Many Ways
Parker E.

My favorite place to motivate me is at youth group. I get to go hang out with other people my age and learn about Christ. I feel like I can tell people about things I am going through there and not get embarrassed at all. I can ask any question and most of the time they will have an answer. If they don't know, we talk about it and see if the Bible tells us anything that might help us find an answer. One question I have asked is, "How did God come into this universe?" The answer is that no one knows. He has always been there.

The most courageous thing I have done is have a full-on conversation with a person who did not know Christ. The person talked about how Mother Nature had made us and created everything. We talked for awhile and she became a Christian. This happened in third grade, which is also when I accepted Jesus Christ as my Savior.

The person who taught me the most about God is my dad. He is so involved with everything I do and has helped me become a Christian.

An experience that showed me how much the world needs saving was when I was 13 years old and went to Pittsburgh, Pennsylvania. I went with my grandma because my great-aunt lives up there. I went on the streets looking for a restaurant to eat at and saw drunk people everywhere. I saw a homeless camp that had to have had 20 tents or more under one bridge. I realized how sad the world is. That experience also taught me how much nicer I need to treat others, because I have no idea what they have been through.

Christina M. Eder

My name is Parker E. I'm in 8th grade and I love Jesus Christ. I love to talk to people and have a good time. I also like video games and trampoline parks.

Look for the Pebbles, Not the Planes
Sarah G.

As a teenager in today's society, I spend quite a bit of time on social media (probably more than I should). In the last few months, I have started watching more Tik Toks, an app where people can upload short videos of themselves doing just about anything.

During this time, I have seen many videos made by Christian creators and many of their words have stuck with me, but one video in particular caught my attention. The clip is a scene from a documentary done by Morgan Freeman.

He is speaking to a woman played by Lauren Graham and they are discussing prayer. It replays in my head every time I ask God for guidance. Morgan Freeman said, "If someone prays for patience, do you think God gives him patience or the opportunity to be patient? If he prayed for courage, does God give him courage or the opportunity to be courageous?"

This stuck with me, because last winter I was confirmed and through that sacrament, you are sealed with the gifts of the Holy Spirit: Wisdom, Knowledge, Understanding, Counsel, Fortitude, Piety and Fear of the Lord. Honestly, I need these. Even though I received them in Baptism, it doesn't mean I always use them.

I am young, so making questionable decisions is part of my daily routine (along with untimely jokes). I realize God is not Santa Claus. Simply by asking Him for something will not make it magically appear.

While this may seem obvious, it was a big discovery for me, one that has completely changed the way I approach prayer and life. Now

Christina M. Eder

when I pray for guidance, I do not look for a plane that's writing answers in the sky. I look for the pebbles (opportunities) God is constantly putting in my path to help me do the next right thing, and ultimately grow closer to Him.

Sarah G. is a high-school student in the great dairy land of America. From her home studio, she works on photography, singing, song writing and growing in knowledge and love for the world around her. She loves cooking, hiking, reading, learning and dancing, whether there is music or not. Sarah is currently working on learning to live life to the absolute fullest and make as many people as possible smile along her way.

Faith Your Fears
Jake I.

One of my favorite things to do on a homeschool day is to explore new places in my neighborhood.

Most days I walk through my backyard, behind my fence. I pass my climbing tree in Mr. Harold's yard, jump off the culvert and follow the creek to a secret forest.

One day I was following the creek behind the house when I came to a fork. The ground was covered with dead leaves and so I wasn't sure about each step.

I went to the left of the fork and it led me to the forest. I had to make my way over a fallen tree through the trees. I found a puddle. Normally it is just a small, dry ditch with rocks. This day, it was a deep puddle, overflowing with water. When it rains the drainage pipe drops into the puddle. It made me think about how things are with God. When he comes into our hearts, we are filled with God and we overflow with good things.

I followed this creek once before. I was surprised the puddle was overflowing. In the past, walking to that puddle scared me. There were times I'd only go so far, but on this day I was having a great day. I decided to take my exploring farther than I have before and took the path.

That puddle has become my secret spot. This experience makes me think about Joshua and how he was called to explore a whole new land.

"The Lord said to Joshua, 'Be strong and courageous. Do not be afraid, do not be discouraged, for the Lord your God will be with you wherever you go' " (Joshua 1:9).

Christina M. Eder

"He turns a desert into pool of water and a dry land into flowing springs" (Psalms 107:35).

My name is Jake, and I am 11 years old. I am home-schooled part time. I love history, Ju jitsu, Legos, reading, biking, exploring and God. I am thankful to live in Tennessee. People are nice and the mountains are beautiful. Other interesting things about me: I was never supposed to be here because my mom wasn't supposed to have me. I love people, a lot!

I've been kinda scared lately because of all the crazy things in our world. Thank you for letting me share this. I want this story to be about courage and strength. I found something that looked like an old forest because the ground was covered with dead leaves. I found much more because I didn't give up. It reminded me to fear not. Faith my fears. When I'm afraid, I will trust God. One step at a time.

God Has a Plan
Aiden J.

"*Did you see that?!*" Caiden shouted.

Caiden, my best friend, and I were on our daily bike ride to the trail not far from our houses. We decided to take the "scenic" route, also known as "go wherever we want and hope we get to our destination."

We were getting lost but having the best time ever. Everything was going well except for one thing, actually getting to the trail. We had been biking for over an hour and were heading away from the trail, knowing we were running out of time. We hightailed it over to the trail and when we got there, we saw the sign that read, "KEEP OUT! CONSTRUCTION AHEAD."

We were mad. We thought that we had just wasted our time, but then realized, "Hey, we just had the best bike ride ever!" We realized, although our plan didn't work, GOD had a plan and His plan is always better, even if we can't see it.

Sometimes I wonder why many people, myself included, try to live their lives thinking, "*Stick to the plan.*" Many times in my life God shows me that though our days might not go according to "our" plan, He always has a plan, whether we like it or not. But whether I realize it or not, his plan is always best.

So, if there are any takeaways from an 11-year-old riding his bike, it would be: GOD HAS A PLAN!

Hello, my name is Aiden, I am 11 years old and I have an older sister. I love playing football. I live in a tiny town called Holmen and love jumping my bike.

Christina M. Eder
Using Gifts to Serve Others
Alia

God calls us to help others in any way we can, using the gifts he has given us.

But how are we supposed to know what said gifts are, and when or how to use them? When I was nearing the end of elementary school, I wanted to help with the church and help people all over, like Mother Teresa. It took a few years to figure out what I needed to do, but during the Covid-19 pandemic, my bandmates and I were presented with a mission.

Back to the beginning...

At the end of the summer, two cousins, my brother and I got together to create a band. We named ourselves *Sunbutt & The Moonshiners*. We were able to do a couple of gigs. Our second gig was an opportunity to open for a local cover band, to help raise money for our school's music department.

This was a great experience because we were able to help our community. During the pandemic, we had more time to see each other and practice. School was still in session and the band wanted to do something to raise money for the lunch program, because they were still serving food to students who needed it.

To decrease the possibility of more Covid-19 cases, we figured it would be best to live stream ourselves playing and have people watching donate online. It looked good on paper, but in practice our idea would not have worked.

My cousins' family had the idea to parade around on a float while playing our music in the neighborhood and collect food for the local food pantry.

The first time we had a parade, we had

tremendous success. The neighborhood was so loving and accepting of this idea. They put bags of non-perishable food items in their driveways for us to pick up and then sat back and watched a group of kids play cover songs.

With the money we gathered from multiple shows, I hope this makes a small impact in our big community. God wants us to help our neighbors and love them so much. This was my way of helping, and I want you to hop right into the water of life, and see what God is calling you to do.

Good luck and *May the Odds be Ever in Your Favor* [a tribute to Suzanne Collins readers].

Salut, my name is Alia. I have two loving parents and a younger brother. I am fluent in sarcasm; I love to read, and enjoy show choir.

Christina M. Eder

A Memory I Will Cherish for Life
Breanna L.

I have learned you can do anything if you put your mind to it. I've learned this through hearing and doing projects with my great-grandfather, Papaw.

My papaw inspired me because he came from a large, poor family with two sisters and four brothers. He joined the National Guard at the age of 15. He wanted to become independent so later he could teach and help his siblings if they needed advice. He stayed in the National Guard until he was 18. He joined the Army after basic training and got stationed in Fort Bliss, Texas.

I think being in Fort Bliss made him become a stronger, independent man. He often had to go out in the desert and spend the night to stand guard. Papaw also practiced firing missiles. He worked on Army trucks in the motor pool. This helped him get a good job in trucking at a company called ABF, so he could provide food for his family. Papaw worked in trucking for 42 years.

My favorite memory I have with Papaw is when he and I rode on the tractor. We'd do garden work and mow the lawn and he always let me drive. I thought it was so fun because my great-grandparents let me drive something so big and expensive when I was only five years old.

Another memory is when it was Papaw's birthday, and we went to Chuck E. Cheese. I got to pick out where we'd go to eat, and he watched me play video games and eat their (what we call) "cardboard pizza."

In fifth grade I had a Veterans Day project to do for English class. I chose to interview Papaw because he's an Army veteran. My project included photos on a poster while Papaw told me all about those trips in the Army.

We also played hopscotch and jumped rope together.

When I was between two and four years old, my grandparents would make me take naps. I would tell Papaw to go lie down, too, so I would take a nap.

Papaw's example helped me learn to be thankful and independent like him. This showed me that I need to help out in my family, get good grades so I can get a good job and succeed in life to be independent.

My name is Breanna. I am in seventh grade and live in Tennessee. I have two loving parents and four dogs. I love spending time with my family, especially on holidays. I love being outdoors and going to the beach. Most of all, I love my Papaw.

Christina M. Eder

God Working
Westley M.

How have you learned how to treat others?
I've learned how to treat others through the Golden Rule: Treat others the way you want to be treated. I try to help others when they are struggling.
I've learned about how to treat others after seeing bullying. One time I took candy from my mom and lied about it. She was mad. I learned you won't get in as much trouble if you just don't steal or lie.

How have you learned about God?
I've learned about God in Sunday school and confirmation. He loves you no matter what you do. I went to a youth conference in Kansas City. That was fun because it wasn't just about studying the Bible, but we got to meet a lot of people from other states. Someone I met was from Arkansas and another was from Hawaii!

How do you see people acting as Jesus would want?
I have a teacher who is really nice and she helps me out. She tells me what I need and how to find it. My mom has also taught me, in that she always believes in me. She encourages me by saying things like "You can do it" and "I know you can."

What makes you believe?
I just keep praying.

What inspires or motivates you?
Sports and racing. It's fun to watch. I get excited and there are different tracks, different cars, and going fast.

What memories have shaped your life?
The memories are from my time with Grandma. She took me places. The first thing

that comes to mind is that we went to rummage sales. I just liked that time we spent together because we always had fun. I also remember our routine during the day when I was younger. She would read to me then take a nap and go for a walk or bake something.

How would you tell someone your age about God who has never heard of God?

I would tell them about the 10 Commandments. If you follow them and the Bible, you will end up in heaven when you die, and he will forgive you if you have made mistakes. He loves you, no matter what.

How do you pray?

I thank God for what I have – my family, health and food. I can get things off my chest, and I feel like I have someone to talk to. I feel him the most when I'm in my room – that feels the most peaceful.

How have you seen God working?

I've prayed for things and He made them happen. It happened on a test that I did really well on.

Where do you see God?

I see God on Christmas. I love the smell of Christmas because my mom puts those scented sticks in the tree so that it smells real. I like being the first one out of bed in the morning to see the tree lit, with presents all around. It feels cozy because the house is clean, but especially when we have snow on the ground.

My name is Westley. I'm 13 years old and live in Wisconsin. I love sports and my family.

Christina M. Eder

Accidental Awakening
Kali V.

My family and I traveled to Morocco in 2015 and I had an unforgettable experience that helped me understand life in a different way. We were there during Eid Al Adha, a special holiday in Morocco where every family slaughters a sheep and has a feast in the streets.

They eat and use all the sheep parts over the course of a few days. My family and I were on a walking tour of the city and saw everything from sheep heads smoking on open fires to children running around wearing sheep intestines like necklaces.

A little girl proudly walked by carrying a severed sheep head; men laid bloody, skinned furs on doorsteps and people sat on stoops, laughing with other family members. Some people were traveling the city with their live sheep on the back of their motorcycle or strapped to their backs!

As an animal lover and vegetarian, I was shocked! It was like nothing we were used to in America, but it was clearly a special day in Morocco and the local people were having great fun! Just like we would celebrate Christmas or Thanksgiving with turkey and come together with family and friends, the people of Morocco were doing the same thing, with their own twist.

For the next few days, people continued cooking sheep parts and throwing parties. I remember walking around and seeing people in open stairwells, roasting kabobs with the final parts of the sheep, or baking sheep horns to turn into new hairbrushes! I was impressed that they let nothing of the sheep go to waste.

The experience taught me that although

cultures are different, holidays are the same and it's all about coming together and celebrating good times. Although I was overwhelmed from the strong smells, the hopeless expressions on the sheep's faces and the runny guts in children's hands, when I look back at it, it was an amazing experience and a reminder to be tolerant of how others live their lives. It was something not many people get to experience, and I wouldn't change it for the world.

Kali V. is a seventh grader at Bearden Middle School in Knoxville, Tennessee. She enjoys writing stories, hanging out with friends and dancing at The Dancers Studio. Kali is a lover of all animals and volunteers at the local Humane Society.

www.ingramcontent.com/pod-product-compliance
Lightning Source LLC
Chambersburg PA
CBHW071849070526
44583CB00016B/1611